Passionately Positive:
The Beverly O'Neill Story

Passionately
Positive:
The Beverly O'Neill Story

Leadership Through Inspiration

HARRY SALTZGAVER

Outskirts Press, Inc.
Denver, Colorado

Contents

Foreword

Beverly O'Neill has been a pivotal person in my life virtually since the day I arrived in Long Beach, California, in 1992.

As the executive editor of a weekly newspaper with a miniscule staff — as in myself and an assistant, at least early on — I found myself following Beverly around. I quickly decided I couldn't keep up.

We met while she was still president of Long Beach City College, but I didn't really get to know her until she ran for mayor. And the fact of the matter is, I didn't get to know her very well then. I was impressed by her love for Long Beach, but feared there was little substance behind the cheerleading.

Further, Beverly had one of those personalities where you wondered if she was too good to be true. She was unfailingly polite, always interested in others' welfare and forever upbeat.

When it comes to politicians, those traits raise the antenna of a newsman. All too often, they have covered colossal egos, sleazy practices and more. I was the new kid in town, and worried that the same was true with Beverly.

Boy, was I wrong.

As she settled in to her job as mayor and I settled in to covering the city I'd end up calling home, we began to build a relationship. She learned that she could trust me to tell both sides of the story and not assume that everyone associated with government was motivated by selfishness. I learned that she had a steel trap for a mind, and creative policies for improving the city she loved.

But I didn't start to know the "real" Beverly until I went to a luncheon for the Flossie Lewis Center, a Long Beach nonprofit agency providing help to women trying to recover from and deal with alcoholism.

Ostensibly, I was there to cover a speech by Paul Williams, the famous songwriter and a Long Beach native son. He delivered an inspirational message, as promised, but the more enlightening part of the program for me was the explanation of who Flossie Lewis was — and the fact that Beverly proudly told the story of her mother Flossie's efforts to help alcoholics.

That revelation forged a bond between Beverly and me, although she didn't know it at the time.

I too, was the child of alcoholic parents. Beverly escaped the genetic predisposition such children have towards alcoholism. I didn't. As they say in Alcoholic Anonymous meeting halls around the world, I was a friend of Bill W.

One trait of children of alcoholic parents is a burning desire to excel. There's an irrational belief that, if you can just be good enough, it will stop the negative actions of your parents (children of divorce sometimes exhibit the same trait). It's irrational because it isn't true. But that doesn't stop us from trying.

I saw that trait in Beverly. I knew I had it, as well. Once I began looking for other similarities, they were myriad. Avoiding confrontation — but fighting ferociously when backed into a corner — seeking to please, finding ways to make peace and believing in the power of redemption; they were all part of Beverly's makeup. I hoped I had some of the same qualities.

Beverly made it all work. What's more, she made it work to the benefit of the entire city.

We connected. I think she could sense I was a kindred soul. I know I could feel her cheering for me as I made a sober life work.

As her third term as mayor marched triumphantly to a close, it became clear to me that there was a book in Beverly's life. Her rise from humble beginnings and the devastation of an alcoholic parent to become the nation's mayor had all the earmarks of an "and they lived happily ever after" movie script.

It also has the advantage of being a true story of overcoming odds, and of telling about the effectiveness of the AA philosophy. It is a philosophy of belief in the ability to positively change a situation, as long as you are willing to accept help and give help along the way.

The biggest challenge to this endeavor has been to not make Beverly sound too good to be true. Without exception, the people interviewed for this book have been huge fans and strong believers in Beverly's sincerity, desire to help others and love for her community.

I confess I count myself among her fans. As a reporter, I pride myself in my ability to objectively present the facts no matter how I personally feel. Once you finish this book, you will undoubtedly say that its author has been biased.

I'll argue that the facts of Beverly O'Neill's life have caused that bias. She's the real deal, and I'm honored to have the chance to share her with you.

Without further ado, here's Beverly.

Introduction — Passionately Positive

Treat people as if they were what they ought to be, and you help them to become what they are capable of being.
—Johann Wolfgang von Goethe

The caravan was crawling from New Orleans to Baton Rouge, Louisiana, to Biloxi, Mississippi, in the first week of September 2005. Beverly O'Neill was going to Biloxi to conduct yet another meeting with mayors of cities and towns devastated by Hurricane Katrina.

O'Neill was there as the mayor of Long Beach, California, and as president of the U.S. Conference of Mayors. She and a small entourage had arrived just 10 days after Katrina hit.

Tom Cochran, executive director of the U.S. Conference of Mayors, and his staff were in the first car. O'Neill, Long Beach Fire Chief Dave Ellis and O'Neill's chief of staff, Cathy Wieder, were in the second car. Others in the small group from California followed in a third vehicle.

"It was a really ravaged area," Wieder said. "It was depressing, to say the least. It was totally devastated.

"Then we literally saw a sign that said Long Beach. It was getting dark, but we knew what was going to happen."

Cochran knew, too. He was already slowing his vehicle down when he saw O'Neill's car pull over.

"I just knew she couldn't pass by," Cochran said. "As soon as I saw the sign, I knew we'd be going there."

"There" was Long Beach, Mississippi, a Gulf Coast town of just more than 17,000 residents, that had been devastated by Hurricane Katrina. More than 90% of the coastal buildings had been destroyed. Many of the residents had no home to return to, and almost none had jobs.

"It was like a ghost town," Wieder remembers. "There was no one around. It took some time to contact anybody."

But Beverly wasn't deterred. Eventually, Long Beach, Mississippi, Mayor William Skellie was tracked down.

"We need to do something here, too," O'Neill said. "We can help, and we will help."

Those 14 words epitomize a lifetime of leadership. From start to finish, one trait has been constant — Beverly O'Neill is, above all, passionately positive.

CHAPTER 1

As a Child

Clarence Lewis moved to Long Beach from South Dakota on the cusp of the Depression. He brought his bride, Flossie, west, hoping to find a living in the oil fields of Signal Hill. Clarence had lost a part of a lung in World War I, though, and acquired a taste for alcohol — not a good recipe for a roustabout.

By the time Flossie found herself pregnant in 1930, friends were asking how she could have a child when her husband was "the way he is." But Clarence landed a job with Shell Oil, and Flossie gave birth to a baby girl with hair nearly as red as her own on September 8, 1930.

As is so often the case with alcoholics, Clarence didn't keep working at any one place for long. Beverly's memories of him from those early days are as sketchy as those of most young children.

"I do remember he would stand me on the bar, and I'd sing," Beverly said. "The men would buy him drinks."

Between trips to the Veterans Administration hospital in Sawtelle and trips into the bottle, Clarence soon couldn't keep his family supported. Clarence wasn't an angry drinker; he was just a drunk.

"My father was not physically abusive," Beverly said. "But there was constant arguing, turmoil and tension. He was just never in control."

That left the raising of Beverly and the supporting of the family to Flossie. In the early 1930s, the options were slim for a woman looking to pay the bills with dignity and still maintain a semblance of normal family life. But the determined young mother found a job at the New Way Laundry; close enough to walk to and from the little apartment on Anaheim Street.

Beverly was 3 years old when Flossie went to work. There was no family to babysit, so Flossie turned to Long Beach Day Nursery for help. It began a connection that remains to this day.

"I'd sit on the porch of the nursery until they opened," Beverly recalls. "For the first couple of years, I'd stay there until mom came to get me. When I was 5, they would walk me to school, and I'd go back to the nursery after school until mom got off work.

"I was there for seven years. It gave me a sense of stability. This was back when women didn't work outside the home, yet everything there was always positive."

That positive feeling didn't reach back to the home. In the constant confusion of an alcoholic's family, Flossie and Beverly closed themselves inside the tiny apartment and stayed there as much as possible.

"On the way to the nursery, we'd walk by a bar called the Blue Heaven, and we'd walk by really fast," Beverly said. "My mother said it was the Black Hell.

"We'd sit in a room in the dark and hope my dad wouldn't come home. I'd never have kids from school over to the house. It was just a very isolated feeling."

Today, Beverly retains the sense of a need for a private space she learned in those early days. She's more than willing to engage in public issues, and is always ready to hear of another's problems, but rarely airs her own personal issues or concerns.

The darkness got even darker as Beverly entered the sixth

grade. Clarence was in the midst of the alcoholic depressive cycle, and had reportedly found a gun.

Flossie took Beverly and moved to Portland, Oregon, for a year. It was a matter of keeping the child safe, but it also was an attempt to try to have Clarence work his problems out for himself.

Finally, Flossie came back. That's what wives were supposed to do in the 1930s and '40s. When it seemed safe, she and Beverly returned to Long Beach.

Flossie would be repaid for her loyalty, but not any time soon. There was more to go through, for both Flossie and Beverly.

There would have to be fire, hot fire, to forge the strong steel these women would become.

CHAPTER 2

Growing Up Early

"In many ways, I always felt like a mother to my mother," Beverly said. "She was a very strong, yet humble, woman. But there were a lot of things about life she didn't understand."

One thing Flossie did understand was that she could rely on Beverly. The two worked out ways to make it through life at a time when women weren't supposed to be able to make it on their own.

Flossie's work schedule didn't leave time to get downtown to pay the bills. So the job fell to Beverly. With a nickel in her hand and a list in her pocket, she would ride the bus downtown to pay the light bill or the gas bill.

"I always got the nickel out before the bus came," Beverly said. "They would recognize me. I'd get there and back with no trouble."

Flossie might have known just what she was doing — creating a task-oriented woman. It didn't hurt that Beverly learned early on that doing things meant controlling the environment around her.

In a 1981 profile of Beverly by Shirley Wild in the *Long Beach Press-Telegram*, Flossie described the bill-paying routine.

"I drew her a map and gave her a list," Flossie said. "Then, as she does now, she went straight down the list, crossing each item off as she accomplished it."

While the home and home life were kept off-limits to the outside world, Beverly was willing to be part of society. She and Flossie became involved with Trinity Baptist Church, and Beverly discovered her love of singing.

Beverly sang as a young child, and when she and her mother returned from Portland, Beverly and Flossie both joined the church choir. Beverly quickly became a soloist. She and Flossie also sang in a small group with one of her school friends, Marlene Rusk, and Marlene's mother.

More than 60 years later, Marlene remembers the redheaded girl who became her role model.

"Beverly never was one for a downer," Marlene (now Temple) said. "She was always friendly. When something needed to be done, she stepped forward.

"She was tall, and I was short, so naturally I looked up to her," Marlene grins. "I am an only child, and I related to Beverly as an older sister. She was always kind and interested in what I was doing. She made me feel very important."

That was the first manifestation of what became a Beverly O'Neill trademark — caring for others and what they cared about. She did it against the background of adversity — an adversity she was able to mask by turning the attention to others.

"I don't think I was ever in their house on Dawson," Marlene said, "even as good of friends as we became. I remember walking past him (Clarence) drunk on the sidewalk. I remember for her it was a matter of acceptance. It was the way life was, and you dealt with it."

Flossie's job at the laundry kept the rent paid and food on the table, but not much else. So when Beverly was 13 (during World War II), she took a job at J.C. Penney's in downtown Long Beach. It added a bit to the home coffers and allowed Beverly to have an occasional new skirt or blouse.

She would keep the job until she was 20 years old, halfway through college.

Beverly, like many children of alcoholics, was an over-achiever who was forever busy. At Trinity Baptist, she worked with the youth groups — she taught Sunday school to Marlene's class — and became the choir director at a young age.

Soon other churches were asking for Beverly's help, both as a singer and a choir director. Beverly and Flossie became the top draw for Mother's Day services with a mother-daughter offering, often with Marlene as an accompanist.

While the music was important, church in those dark days meant much more, Beverly says.

"It was an anchor for us," she says. "We prayed for my dad. Our faith gave us hope. What do you do with a life out of control? You give it to a higher power."

Flossie taught by example, and that included spiritual teaching. She gave Beverly the middle name of Joy, and said often that she had turned Beverly over to God.

"In a sense, our faith was our hope," Beverly said. "We would feel that someone was watching over us. Church was very personal for us."

That faith wasn't just a matter of sitting back and waiting for God to make everything better, though.

"I strongly believe that God helps those who help themselves," Beverly said. "If I'm not prepared for an opportunity, that's my fault."

It is a lesson often repeated in the world of Alcoholics Anonymous. You rely on a higher power, but you have to do the work, too. Beverly was nothing if not a worker — a worker with faith.

CHAPTER 3

Preparing For The Miracle

"I wouldn't wish being a child in an alcoholic family on anyone," Beverly says. "You live in fear, turmoil and anxiety. The rate of alcoholism (in the children) is high. It was my mother who really saved me. But I do think I was old, even as a little girl."

On the outside, Beverly was friendly and involved. In addition to her job at Penney's and her church choir efforts, she was asked to sing at Loper's Funeral Parlor, with funerals scheduled around her lunch hour so she could make it.

But Beverly remembers herself as shy and quiet. The open secret of her father's condition meant a large portion of her life was not to be shared.

"I grew up as a fly on the wall," she says. "I didn't play. It was just my mom and I. We had a great bond, but ... it was lonely."

Bill Barnes, a high school friend whose life paralleled Beverly's through a career in education, remembers her a little differently, at least in high school.

"She was more quiet than shy," Barnes said. "She was very popular."

As she entered her senior year at Poly High School, Beverly's life began to change. She found herself in Miss Gridley's English class with Bill O'Neill, the confident and smart president of the senior class.

"I thought he was just the best," Beverly says. "The bee's knees, if you will. And he noticed me."

One glance at a picture from high school explains Bill's interest. Beverly's nickname was "Legs," and the tall redhead was nothing if not striking.

As seems to be inevitable in the case of high school romance, things weren't smooth. As Bill escorted Beverly home on their first date, they stepped off the bus at Cherry Avenue and Anaheim Street.

"There was Dad, asleep on the bus bench," Beverly recalls. "He was drunk. I didn't say a word, but after Bill said goodbye, I ran home."

Flossie was struggling, too. She had been married to Clarence for 24 years. She had always said, when asked why she stayed, that she was determined to be married for 25 years so everyone would know she gave the marriage a good try.

It was hard.

"But my mom had an answer," Beverly says. "She always said to have faith that someday it would be all right."

Faith or not, Flossie wasn't one to sit back and wait. She had heard of a new program called Alcoholics Anonymous. She sent a letter asking for more information to a post office box she had found in a story in The Saturday Evening Post about the group.

To her surprise, the response came from an address down the street. It was from the woman who owned the store there — a liquor store.

Flossie's response was recorded in a 1977 interview by Barbara Bradley published in the *Press-Telegram*.

"She called and said she had my letter," Flossie said. "But I was mad at her for selling liquor to my husband, and I thought, 'you nosy gal.' I wasn't even polite.

"When she told me her husband was a member of AA, I

almost fainted. I never thought they had an alcohol problem, too. I thought we were the only ones in the world with the problem."

Clarence didn't know it then, but his drinking days were numbered. The sun had begun to shine in Flossie's and Beverly's lives.

CHAPTER 4

The Miracle of Sobriety

"My mother caught on first as to what AA was," Beverly says. "She always said she'd turn him black and blue when they went to meetings, she'd nudge him so much."

Alcoholics Anonymous was in its own infancy, especially on the West Coast, when Clarence and Flossie began attending meetings in 1945. The group claims 1935 as its birthday, with Bill W. and others forming the first group in Ohio. Ten years later, there still was no organized help for families of alcoholics, and little formal help at all for alcoholics in Long Beach.

Still, with Flossie's support (and her poking and prodding), Clarence got sober, and stayed that way for a year. He slipped — a monumental binge, according to Beverly — but quickly returned to the AA fold. He would remain sober the rest of his life, and become a pillar of the AA movement in Long Beach.

Beverly didn't know what the future held for her father, though. She was a teenager who had known nothing but a father who couldn't care for himself, let alone care for her.

"I remember her saying that as soon as she graduated from high school, she was going to leave home," Marlene says. "She was sad because she said she couldn't ever have a church wedding, because he wouldn't be able to walk her down the aisle."

Beverly remembers her disbelief when her father first stopped drinking.

"I was skeptical when he first started to try," she says. "But when he went to meetings, I started to admire him."

Which made it all the more difficult when Clarence "went out," in AA vernacular, and drank again.

"When he slipped after a year, we really tiptoed around," Beverly says. "But my mom hung in there, and after he got sober again, he never turned back."

Many would say that Flossie wouldn't let him turn back. She is known as the mother of Al-Anon in Southern California, the support group created for families of alcoholics. Flossie never had a drink in her life, and while Beverly has an occasional glass of wine with dinner, she has the same attitude about alcohol in general.

"I never wanted to be addicted to something where I'd have no control over myself," she says. "I thought if you can't have self-discipline and succumb to it (addiction), there was something wrong. But I came to see it differently. AA was life changing. They were doing it with discipline, and with help.

"I learned that everyone has their own bottom, whether it's waking up on the lawn to turning tricks to being jailed. The thing is, you realize you have to change or you're going to die."

Beverly used that same lesson when she became mayor of Long Beach at a dark time in the city's life. But that's getting ahead of the story. There were family triumphs first.

Flossie decided that the best way to keep Clarence in the program was to bring the program into their home. The first AA 24-hour hotline in Long Beach was in the Lewis household, and that home became the de facto central office for the area when Beverly was a senior in high school. It would be a 24-hour-a-day reality for all of the Lewises for the next five years.

History would prove that the daily lessons of AA would turn out to be one of the most important schools Beverly ever attended.

CHAPTER 5

Lessons To Be Learned

"When Bill and I were dating, he'd bring me home and ask where my parents were," Beverly says. "They were always at meetings. We were very involved in AA, but no one knew about it. It was, after all, supposed to be anonymous."

The Lewis household might have been anonymous to the general public, but it was well known in the community of Alcoholics Anonymous members and those who dealt with alcoholics. The only detoxification centers in the late 1940s were the police station holding cells, and the concept of recovery centers had yet to be invented.

So Clarence and Flossie opened their home to those in need (Clarence had begun working steadily again, and the family lived in a house with a garage — and no car). Police dropped off those they thought might be helped more by a stay in the Lewis garage than in the city jail, and Flossie opened her house to women with the same problem.

It fell to Beverly (who lived at home while she attended Long Beach City College and California State University, Long Beach) to help answer the phone and help with the "visitors" when her parents weren't available.

"It was the biggest eye-opener of my life," Beverly says. "It gave me an appreciation of what my father went through. To see the willpower and strength that these people had to totally change their lives was so inspirational."

While Beverly got to see the miracle of recovery, she also saw the heartbreak of despair so deep it destroyed lives. She talks of one such experience as if it occurred yesterday.

"My folks had gone to a meeting and I had a call," she says. "The woman said she wanted to talk to my mom. I told her my mom would be back later, but she asked if she could come over then. Of course I said yes.

"She was a lovely, tall, stylish blonde. We talked for at least three hours. She was a teacher, but her daughter was back east because she didn't think she could take care of her because of her (the teacher's) drinking.

"When she left, I remember thinking how I felt she had everything to live for. But two weeks later, I read that she had committed suicide in a rundown public restroom.

"It really affected me. She felt she had lost everything because she had lost control, and took the easiest way out."

Learning to not take the easy way out was a painful, but important, lesson. Beverly had learned early on that recognition of a problem is the first step to solving that problem. The second step is to confront the issue directly; avoid avoiding it, so to speak.

Still, Beverly — true to her character — found it easier to focus on the more positive lessons. The successes offered hope.

"I think people have the capacity to change their lives," she says. "No one wants to live as a failure. Some of them just don't know how to live in a positive way. When you can help them do that, well, it doesn't get much better than that."

Beverly made it her life's work to find that feeling as often as possible. Many people have benefited from that quest.

Clarence would stay sober for more than 18 years, until his death in 1965. When the National Council on Alcoholism conducted its 1986 annual meeting in Long Beach, it hosted the Clarence J. Lewis Annual Awards Banquet.

Clarence and Flossie gave up operating the Harbor Area AA central office out of their home shortly after Beverly graduated from college, but remained integral parts of the Long Beach AA community — so much so that one of the first recovery homes for women in the city was named the Flossie Lewis Recovery Center.

"I learned there are talents in everyone," Beverly says. "You just have to be accepting to get them to the point where they succeed. I learned from my mother how important it is to help people help themselves. I tried to take that to all my jobs."

CHAPTER 6

The Butterfly Emerges

Clarence was able to go back to work fairly steadily when Beverly was a senior in high school, as he began his journey into sobriety. The family still didn't have much money (and Beverly continued to both work at Penney's and as a choir director), but a sense of normalcy began to surface.

"It was so wonderful that Mom was home when I got home from school," Beverly says. "Dad started doing pretty well and we moved to the house on Molino (which became the Harbor Area AA Central Office). She just jumped into the AA life with both feet."

It probably was no coincidence that Beverly found more confidence in her own life in that time as well. For example, when she met and fell for Poly's class president, Bill O'Neill, she decided to do something about it.

"I thought he was the cutest, smartest thing I'd ever seen," Beverly says. "He's still the smartest man I've ever known. I asked him to the backwards dance (sometimes known as the Sadie Hawkins dance)— the one where the girls asked the boys — and he said yes. I remember I brought him a decorated potato as a corsage."

Bill and Beverly didn't "go steady." They had a broader picture of the world, Beverly says. But there was a mutual interest, one that would culminate in marriage in 1952.

But there was an education to be gained first. And despite the budding romance with Bill, Beverly remained largely in her shell in high school, not joining clubs or running for any class positions. In retrospect, she admits that reluctance likely resulted from her home life.

"The biggest thing I did in high school was getting the lead in 'The Mikado' my senior year," Beverly says. "And meeting Bill. That's how it was."

Bill Barnes grins when he talks about the dynamic leader Beverly became and compares her with the high school Beverly.

"When we were growing up, Bill was the politician, not her," Barnes said. "But I could tell she had something special."

Like many high schoolers, Beverly didn't realize how quickly she was maturing. She found herself the star in the high school musical, one of the most popular and accomplished young men in school was on her arm, and she was dealing with very adult situations at home.

As Beverly ventured out into the college world, confidence could hardly fail to grow.

The Poly High School class of 1948 joined a country reveling in the victorious end of World War II. The boys came marching home to take over jobs and go to college, and institutions of higher education expanded rapidly to accommodate the demand. Treatises have been written on how the creation of the GI Bill democratized higher education, and Beverly and Bill were more than happy to take advantage.

"We both went to Long Beach City College," Beverly says. "It's what we could do in our city and what we could afford."

Beverly had made it to college. She began to feel more at ease with herself, and the realization she could make a difference for those around her.

She was studying music education at City College, so she decided to run to become the arts representative on the associated students governing body.

"I realized I had something, some ability to help people work together," Beverly says. "I ended up being president of the Women Students (Association) there."

She would later follow that by being elected president of the Associated Women Students at California State University, Long Beach. She and Bill were among the pioneering students who helped shape that university in its very first years — CSULB opened in 1949, Beverly and Bill enrolled in 1950. A positive, "let's get it done" approach characterized her leadership style even then.

Beverly didn't know it at the time, but she had many of the traits common to children of alcoholics (those studies were still in the future). She was an over-achiever with a near obsession for being in control of her own fate. She was calm in the face of adversity, willing to work the issue out instead of panic or flee.

The desire to avoid conflict, a bedrock trait of children of alcoholics, can cause people to retreat from life or avoid confrontation at all costs. Beverly took the trait's positive trail — becoming a facilitator of consensus.

"I always wanted to please people, to bring people together. If there was anything I hate, it is an argument. My early life was full of that," she says. "I found out at LBCC that I was a hugger. I worked for people to be pleasant to one another; I tried to encourage people to work through things."

Beverly graduated from CSULB in 1952 with a bachelor's degree in music education and a teacher's certificate. In the same period, Bill had earned a BA in history and a master's degree in English.

"When I was at Long Beach State, that was a miracle in itself," Beverly said. "I always thought that you had to either be brilliant or rich to go to college... But there I was."

Graduation in May 1952 was a landmark. Neither Flossie

nor Clarence had finished high school — Beverly was a college graduate with a credential that said she could start teaching.

"My mother could have done all sorts of things if she would have had the opportunity," Beverly says. "Now I had that opportunity. It is a feeling I have never forgotten."

That feeling and a desire to give it to others would guide Beverly 15 years later, at Long Beach City College when she started the Women's Center. But there was some life to live first, and a young couple looking forward to living it.

CHAPTER 7

Into The World

Beverly Lewis became Beverly O'Neill on Christmas 1952. It was one of the biggest weddings of the year at Our Savior's Lutheran Church, and one Beverly hadn't thought possible. She tears up every time she tells the story.

"We invited the small Cal State faculty, and put up a notice on the AA bulletin board," she says. "When the day came, there were more than 500 people there.

"I never dreamed of a church wedding. I never thought my dad could walk me down the aisle. Yet there I was, and there he was. It was amazing. We were all crying."

Bill and Beverly paid for their own wedding — Clarence was doing better, but there certainly was no money for a dowry. Flossie and Clarence spent much of their energy on AA activities in Long Beach, even after the central office really became an office instead of the Lewis household.

"Mom and Dad never had any money to give me," Beverly said. "The last conversation I had with my Dad, he said he was sad he hadn't left me anything that was good. I told him, 'you stopped drinking, and you gave me a life with you. You let me finish school. You gave me everything — you gave me the tools to have a future'."

Beverly had landed a job teaching kindergarten in the Long Beach school district. Bill, who had joined the Navy Reserve, was activated for the Korean conflict and went to serve shortly after the couple was married.

In addition to teaching, Beverly continued to serve as choir director at her church, Trinity Baptist, and assistant director at a Methodist church. She also helped her parents with their AA activities. It was an energy level that would be one of her trademarks throughout her life.

Clarence had been sober for more than five years, and his dream was to have a service station of his own. But his history stood in his way.

"Dad could never borrow any money because he didn't have credit, so I bought them a used car," Beverly says. "After I'd been working for awhile, I borrowed $1,100 from the Long Beach School District Credit Union so he could start his own gas station. Mom learned to drive in her 50s, and was using the car to go everywhere, like it was a new world. Dad was in his station at Seventh and Junipero. It was great."

Bill came home in 1954. He had the GI Bill and a dream — to use his GI benefit to study overseas for a year to learn French and German for his Ph.D. The young couple headed for Vienna, where Bill did graduate work in languages and philosophy. Beverly took art and music classes. The GI Bill was enough for the couple to live on.

"It was just incredible," Beverly says. "What an experience it was. Another miracle, to be sure."

Returning to Long Beach in 1955, Bill also took a job with the Long Beach Unified School District and worked to complete his doctorate at the University of Southern California. Beverly returned to the elementary school classroom, and worked on her master's degree at Long Beach State.

In 1957, Beverly received her master's degree, Bill received his Ph.D., and both moved to higher education — Bill as a professor of educational psychology at Long Beach State, Beverly as a teacher and counselor at Compton Community College.

The couple started something else about the same time. Her name was Teresa, and she was born on Nov. 14, 1958.

Beverly didn't feel that she could (or wanted to) become a stay-at-home mom. She recalled those days in her childhood when there wasn't ever enough money.

"We were barely making ends meet," Beverly says. "I was always afraid something would happen. That's why I got every credential I could. I couldn't see not being prepared to work."

Childcare was as scarce in the late 1950s as it had been in the 1930s. But for Beverly, there was an alternative to the Long Beach Day Nursery — Grandma Flossie.

"When Bill and I bought our first house, it was a duplex so we could always have my parents close," Beverly says. "… I told her I'd pay her what she would have earned working outside to take care of Teresa. She was so thrilled. It was like having a second chance (for Flossie to mother a child)."

Second chances are what Alcoholics Anonymous is all about. Second chances, and making the most of those chances with the help and support of those around you, that is. Beverly was becoming an expert at both sides of that equation.

Beverly at age 10 with Flossie.

Teresa at age 8 with
Grandma Flossie.

Beverly at 19 singing at an early AA meeting.

An iconic family portrait from the early 1950s, with Clarence reading the Big Book.

With pearls and gloves, Beverly walks with Teresa.

Flossie, in her New Way Laundry uniform, walks with Beverly.

One of the few pictures of Clarence with a young Beverly.

Beverly walks to receive her doctorate degree at USC.

CHAPTER **8**

A Family Affair

By the time Teresa started attending Lowell Elementary School in Long Beach, both Beverly and Bill had settled in at institutions where they would spend most of their professional careers. Bill joined the University of Southern California School of Education as a professor. Beverly transferred to Long Beach City College, teaching music and filling the position of Woman's Advisor. The move was simple, since at that time the two-year community college was part of the Long Beach Unified School District.

Bill quickly became immersed in academia, ultimately authoring eight books, creating and guiding international education outreach programs, chairing the Department of Social and Philosophical Foundations of Education and more. Teresa calls Beverly and Bill the ultimate Type A parents — successful, active and trying to make a difference. Both Beverly and Teresa say they sympathize with Bill living in a world inhabited by a trio of highly energetic women.

Two passions kept Flossie, Beverly and Teresa bonded closely together — music and work with alcoholics and families of alcoholics. Teresa became Flossie's sidekick in many of her efforts to help others.

"Nana lived 'downstairs' for most of my life," Teresa says. "I remember she always seemed to have bright yellow cars. We were always going around giving people stuff. Her car was always full of clothes and toys for families.

"She taught me what it was like to be comfortable with yourself. She was a character. She'd go to the cemetery to take naps. She said people would think she was passed out with grief. She just thought it was a convenient place to nap.

"I just remember how great it was to hang out with her."

Flossie and Beverly's tradition of public singing was passed on to Teresa at an early age. She learned to play an auto harp early in elementary school, and the duo became a trio.

"As three generations of women, we were the hottest act around on Mother's Day," Teresa said. "I loved it. Mom and grandma showed me how to show people you care."

Teresa followed Beverly's path through Long Beach schools, deviating slightly by graduating from Wilson High instead of her mother and father's alma mater, Poly High. She also found pleasure in performing, going into the theater department in high school and becoming a cheerleader when she started at Long Beach City College.

When it was time to transfer to a four-year school, Teresa opted for USC and its renowned film school. By that time, both of her parents had earned doctorate degrees from USC — Beverly had spent five years doing her doctoral work nights and weekends while fulfilling her duties at LBCC. She would become Dr. O'Neill in 1977.

"I was less active in clubs and activities (in college) than she was," Teresa says of her mother. "She was always very supportive. She taught me that if I made up my mind to do something and worked at it, I could do it. She was never negative."

That positive support — along with the philosophy that it didn't matter if you were a woman or a man if you could do the job — helped Teresa find a career. She had a master's degree in professional writing and had found work as an assistant on the television sitcom "Love, Sidney." She assisted the writers, but wanted more.

"There were not many women in the field," she says. "But I figured, 'Why not me?' I had watched my mother break through that glass ceiling. So I just quit my job and stayed in my apartment writing scripts.

"There was never any form of discouragement from either of my parents, although I'm sure they wondered what I was doing. I remember calling and just crying because I was scared. She convinced me I had to try it."

It worked. The popular series "Night Court" picked up one of Teresa's scripts, and ultimately made her one of its primary writers. She has since had credits on "Home Improvement," "Coach" and other shows.

Teresa continues to write, but can't get away from the family's legacy of educating. She now teaches writing part-time at USC in the Master of Professional Writing program.

"I started teaching at USC in 2000," Teresa says. "The first class I had, I was in the same building where my dad taught. That was something."

CHAPTER **9**

The Age of Aquarius

By the mid-1960s, Beverly's career began to take a path towards administrative leadership. She still taught music — her first love — but began to find more fulfillment as the women's advisor.

"I started teaching College and Career Opportunities for Women in 1967," Beverly says. "There was so much need, and all of a sudden I found myself in a job as women's advisor, where I could do things for women of all ages."

The tenor of the times had a lot to do with Beverly's path. The freewheeling, tumultuous '60s had a number of long-lasting social impacts that would change American life for generations, perhaps permanently. One key change was a new empowerment of women. The females attending LBCC no longer were exclusively teenagers continuing their educations.

"I started the class with those women with children in day care," Beverly says. "I remember thinking how my mother could have done all sorts of things if she had had the opportunity. I wanted to give these women the opportunity to explore the possibilities.

"There were those who were re-entering the workforce. They had spent 20 years growing up, then 20 years raising a family. Now it was, 'What were they supposed to do now?'"

Betty Freidan's "The Feminine Mystique" was published in 1963 and had expanded women's horizons and expectations. The birth control pill and the sexual revolution had diminished, if not eliminated, the one-sided social attitude about sexuality, making women equal to men in that arena.

But there were down sides to both of the new freedoms. Women were expected to be tough and compete in a business world that still was nowhere near a level playing field. Sexual parity brought with it an increase in the divorce rate that left women — often with families — suddenly alone and struggling.

So in 1969, the same year she became dean of LBCC's liberal arts campus, Beverly founded the Women's Resource Center, then known as the Continuing Education Center for Women. She says she tried to instill a simple philosophy — "It isn't what happens to you, it's what you do about it."

"We weren't doing anything other than what the college was doing already — preparing students for life," Beverly says. "So many of these women also thought that to go to college you had to be either rich or brilliant or 18, and we had to get past that."

Beverly brought Freidan to Long Beach to speak in 1966. But she wasn't interested in an activist role for herself. Even then, Beverly says, she believed in making a difference rather than making noise or trying to make an impression.

"This was not a feminist center," Beverly says. "It was women helping women. It was not a bra-burning bunch. It was women trying to build some kind of future independently."

Money for the center was scarce, and it was staffed mainly by volunteers. Even though Beverly's plate was increasingly filled with administrative duties, she continued her personal involvement, and continued to teach the career opportunities class.

High school friend Bill Barnes had also focused on education, and reunited with Beverly as colleagues at LBCC. He says the impression she made was important.

"Beverly's vision of the women's center was right on the cusp, the cutting edge," Barnes said. "She modeled what she was teaching, and the women believed in her."

For Beverly, the payoff was in the people.

"By the late 1960s, displaced housewives were much more prevalent (as students at LBCC)," Beverly says. "I remember one woman whose husband had died. She had tried to commit suicide twice. She couldn't drive, she didn't know how to handle a bank account.

"But she came back to school, and eventually she became the night desk manager at a large hotel. She changed her life. That was so wonderful. That's what we were there for."

The center offered a second chance, and help to make that second chance a success. If that sounds familiar, it should.

As is always the case, Beverly's own experience colored the lessons she taught to others. She had known despair as a child of an alcoholic, and saw what her mother had done about it. She summed up what she had learned in an interview with Edward Ogle for his 2000 doctoral dissertation.

"When you put things in the proper order, despair doesn't help you," Ogle quotes Beverly. "You have to look at what you can do about a situation and don't wallow in despair. It is not healthy or productive."

Beverly's belief in the power of the individual, learned through her experiences with members of Alcoholics Anonymous, played a large part in her approach to the center and those who used its services. Jan Foster, who became coordinator of the Women's Resource Center in 1980, explained Beverly's impact to Shirley Wild for a 1981 story in the Long Beach Review.

"Beverly completely changed my life," Foster said. "She's genuinely interested in people and their personal growth. Her warmth makes people feel very special."

Beverly's interest in helping women re-enter the world took a scholarly path, as well. Her own doctoral dissertation detailed the efforts of women trying to re-enter the workforce through LBCC from 1969 to 1976 and how institutions of higher learning could best serve those women.

Beverly knew the importance of what she and her volunteers had created. In a 1979 interview in the *Press-Telegram* about the center, she said:

"Beginning the women's center and watching it grow has probably been the most satisfying experience of my professional career."

Today, the center is called the Women and Men's Resource Center, and provides everything from housing and employment information to parenting referrals and crisis counseling, with offices on both campuses.

"I thought the women's center wouldn't last more than 10 years," Beverly says today. "But it has gone forward and grown with the times — almost 40 years. That's something."

CHAPTER 10

In The Ivory Tower

In 1971, two years after starting the Women's Center, the position of Dean of Student Affairs became available. Beverly was asked to apply. The only condition she had was that she be allowed to continue teaching and overseeing the center.

Once in the job, Beverly concentrated on strengthening the student affairs program, including the structure for student government, expanding student service programs, consolidating student bodies over the two campuses and establishing a uniform fee program. She also had direct responsibility for all varsity sports, recreation, intramural programs, and all clubs and organizations.

"Athletics are vitally important to college life," Beverly says. "It's a non-threatening way to build pride and enthusiasm. As far as I'm concerned, anything that keeps students in school is worth it."

She found ways to help students grow both as people and as students, according to Wells Sloniger, her colleague at City College and a self-professed mentee.

"I tried to be like Bev," Sloniger said. "When she hired me (as Dean of Men), I was working for a woman for the first time in my life. She helped shape me as a person, and I watched her do the same with a lot of other people."

Beverly worked with individuals, but looked to the big picture as well. She passionately believed in the importance of student activities and services, and thought that the lack of student centers on both campuses was holding LBCC back.

"I went to Jim Gray, who was president of the LBUSD school board at the time," Beverly recalls. "I told him we needed a student center. Before we were through, we had two (one at each campus). Both were designed by local architects, too – Dick Poper and Dwight Bennett."

In her six years as Dean of Student Affairs, Beverly directed the design, construction and even the furnishing of the College Center on the Liberal Arts Campus and the design and re-modeling of the outdated Student Center on the Pacific Coast campus.

She also began honing the caring, individual-oriented style of management she later became famous for: management by walking around. Sloniger calls it management through caring.

"She established trust with everyone she worked with," Sloniger said. "You got to where you wanted to please the boss. The more you did for her, the more she appreciated it, and the more you wanted to do for her.

"She is a good listener. She made you know she cared. I think it was her best quality."

Today, Beverly describes the way she likes to lead as facilitative management — bringing people together. In a 2009 speech about her career, she was asked to define a leader.

"It's someone who inspires others to work together on a common vision," she responded.

The simple fact is, she says, people work harder at something if they believe in what they are doing.

"People work tirelessly when they have a strong commitment to the task," Beverly says. "I've seen people who are demanding and people who only give lip service to the buy in. Demanding people don't really care whether anyone else likes it.

"I've always wanted people to feel they are succeeding as a person. You're not going to get there by demanding. You have to work together for a common goal."

While Beverly refuses the mantle of female pioneer, she admits she was aware that she was breaking new ground as she moved up the ranks at City College. She was the first woman to be dean of student affairs at LBCC, let alone vice president of student services or superintendent/president.

"I felt it was important that I take the steps," Beverly says. "Women simply weren't as visible in leadership roles."

It also put Beverly in a position of working predominately with men, either as peers or as subordinates. She seldom admits it, but those around her say she seems to enjoy working with men to this day.

"All of the committees, internally and externally, were male-dominated," Sloniger said. "She got on a lot of boards because of what she could do, but she was still a woman. She had to prove herself a lot."

When Beverly was chosen as vice president of student services in 1977, Sloniger followed her up the ladder to become dean of students. From there, he watched as Beverly polished her leadership skills without giving up her principle of being positive about people.

"She would treat everyone with the same respect and concern," Sloniger said. "Everyone got the same attention, the same feeling that she cared. People knew they could approach her.

"Her mom had a way of helping people all the time. She saw that and tried to emulate it. She said that you don't write people off because they made a mistake. And she lived it."

That kind of approach inspired loyalty. It also was laying the groundwork for Beverly's future as the woman who could bring all of Long Beach together.

CHAPTER 11

Madame President

"When I became president (in 1988), it was heresy," Beverly said. "I heard things like, 'I hope she doesn't cry.' But it was a change in all of society, for women to take positions of responsibility... I felt it was important to take the job."

That sort of challenge was like a clarion call to Beverly, according to her long-time colleague, Sloniger.

"She confided in me once that maybe she was one generation ahead of her time," Sloniger said. "But she wanted others to have a chance, and she knew that to make that happen, she had to take the chances herself."

Actually, Beverly says, that was Sloniger's (and others') perception. She saw the job as president/superintendent as a logical progression. She had applied for the position the last time it was open, and was quick to apply again.

"I went after it," she said. "I did it because I had been vice president for 10 years, and had been part of City College for many years. I thought it was a position where I could accomplish some things.

"There's a saying I believe in — when opportunity meets preparation, that's good luck."

Beverly has created good luck her entire life – for herself and those around her. She made sure she was prepared to do her job, and to help others do theirs.

Beverly had already made a name for herself in Long Beach, and immediately became more visible as LBCC president. She believed in personally supporting others' efforts, and just stepped that up in her new position.

"She was always involved in the community," Sloniger said. "She truly loved Long Beach. I used to be her driver to functions. She had great energy. If you didn't have energy, you couldn't keep up with her.

"She helped build college relationships with the city. She felt she had to be at everything. That's where she developed relationships."

Shortly after becoming president, Beverly initiated talks with then-LBUSD Superintendent Tom Giugni and CSULB President Steve Horn (and later, the next CSULB president, Bob Maxson) to create something Beverly called articulation between the institutions. The idea was to eliminate roadblocks as students progressed through school.

It was yet another example of Beverly bringing people together to work for a common goal. This time, the goal was nothing less than getting Long Beach students from kindergarten through university (if they wanted to go), all in Long Beach.

Put another way, she put her institution, City College, in the role she saw for herself — facilitating success for others. Start with proper preparation from the public schools, add alignment of academic credits between LBCC and CSULB, and that provided the opportunity for a university degree.

Carl Cohn took over at LBUSD two years after Beverly retired as president at LBCC and helped expand the concept even further. The program became formalized, with written agreements between the institutions. Named Seamless Education by CSULB Provost Karl Anotol, the program has grown over the last 18 years and continues to be a signature Long Beach program. Beverly continued to support the effort throughout her mayoral career, and people point to it as part of her legacy.

The Seamless Education model has been cited as one reason LBUSD has been a finalist each year it has been eligible for the Broad Prize for excellence in urban education. The district has won the award once — during Beverly's tenure as mayor. She was there in Washington, D.C., in 2003, beaming like the proud parent she was, when the Broad Prize was handed to Superintendent Chris Steinhauser.

Most importantly, it provided a framework for people to help themselves. It broadened Beverly's concept of the Women's Center to include all students, from start to finish, and she still gets credit for the innovative idea today.

"She was the driving force behind Seamless Education," said Judy Seal, currently the executive director of the Long Beach Education Foundation and coordinator of the seamless education effort for the Long Beach Unified School District, LBCC and CSULB. Seal was part of the effort from near the beginning.

The effort reached a peak in 2008 with "The Long Beach College Promise," a promise made by LBCC and CSULB that all eligible students in Long Beach would get a college education, including a semester of tuition free of charge at LBCC and guaranteed admission at CSULB. The agreement reached between LBUSD Superintendent Chris Steinhauser, LBCC President Eloy Oakley and CSULB President F. King Alexander was the first of its kind, and has become a national model.

That's collaboration of the O'Neill kind.

It all started from one woman deciding it might be a good idea to get some people together with a common goal — helping the community she loved by helping people succeed.

CHAPTER **12**

The Leader

Beverly describes her leadership style as facilitative. She said she tries to bring people together behind a common vision, and then facilitate ways to get things done.

And it is relentlessly positive.

"When I first became mayor, I was afraid I needed to be a table pounder," Beverly said. "I'm not a table pounder, I'm a talker, a consensus-finder. Any office I had, any success I achieved, that's how it was done."

Coworkers invariably talk about being part of Beverly's team. Sloniger said she perfected the team approach as president of LBCC. She did it, he said, by treating everyone warmly, with respect and genuine concern.

"She had strong student organizations," Sloniger said. "She had a way of giving students another chance if they made a mistake, and that made them want to do better for her."

The second chance, one day at a time philosophy of AA surfaces again here, as does the belief that people can succeed when given that chance, along with support and guidance. She cared.

"Being caring, the way I experienced it from Bev, meant action on her part," Judy Seal said. "It meant that she would call me and ask, "How's it going? Let's go over this; Have you hit any road-blocks?;' Things like that. And it was always positive."

Whether it came naturally or it was learned, Beverly's positive approach — gentle encouragement coupled with supportive and enlightened advice — inspired confidence.

Finding the common goal is a key to leading any group, Beverly says. She recalled one issue early in her presidency that helped unite the student body behind her.

City College's liberal art campus is bisected by Carson Street, a major thoroughfare. When Beverly became president, there was only one traffic signal at one end of campus.

"We led the charge with the students, and we got a stop sign on Carson for safety," she recalled. "We also got a parking lot on the corner.

"It wasn't that big an issue. But it created a sense of unanimity among the students, the faculty and the staff. That, in turn, helped everyone feel better about the institution."

Big deal or not, Beverly took her trademark approach to the issue. First she brought the people who saw the problem together to brainstorm. She synthesized their concepts to come up with an action plan, involving people all along. Then came the meeting with the people — all the people — necessary to put the plan in place.

Step by step, the objective is achieved.

As with any strong leader, Beverly has a unique personal charisma, a trait she typically denies. But the response by those she leads makes it apparent, Barnes said.

"I marveled at how she worked with people, how skilled she was at moving an agenda," he said. "Her leadership was based on trust. She was able to project an agenda, and make it the product of others. People didn't question her intentions. They knew she was doing it because it was the right thing for them, for the institution."

Beverly translated the best traits associated with being a woman into being a leader, Sloniger said. Her concern for people's problems translated into improvements in the jobs being done.

"She never let titles get in the way," he said. "She didn't have an ego, and didn't appreciate others trying to promote their own egos at the expense of others. It was about worth. She gave volunteers, employees, everyone their own business cards, for example. She believed everyone should feel good about themselves and their contributions."

Beverly tells a story that adds a nuance to her effort to value everyone. It starts with a custodian who came to her when she was president. He was extremely upset, ready to quit his job. He was a longtime employee the college didn't want to lose. So Beverly tried to find out what was causing the dissatisfaction.

"It turned out the gardeners were kicking cigarette butts onto the sidewalk (out of flowerbeds)," she said. "It might seem like nothing to us, but it was important to him. It provided such a message about how relevant and irrelevant things are to different people.

"I listened and I empathized with him. I told him, 'I can see how you are feeling about this because you are obviously so upset and so emotional about this issue. It is something that we can take care of.'" (From "The Art of Winning Commitment," Dick Richards, 2004)

An abundance of that empathy stood Beverly in good stead throughout her career. Some observers occasionally translated that caring into an inability to make a tough decision, but invariably found out they were mistaken.

"You have to be able to say, 'If I were in your shoes, I might feel the same way," Beverly said. "But in my shoes, I have to take into consideration this, this and this. I really understand how you are feeling, but I have to be responsible for more than just that (that person's perspective)." (Same source)

Compassion with strength was Beverly's hallmark at City College, Sloniger said. It clearly came from her upbringing.

"Her mom had a way of helping people all the time, sometimes just by listening, sometimes by providing more," Sloniger said. "She saw that, and saw a way to make that approach her own. Her mother was her inspiration."

Flossie was strong inspiration. Beverly was a master at putting that inspiration to work, from leading LBCC through leading Long Beach.

CHAPTER **13**

Transition

"I was 63, and I'd been president for five years," Beverly said of her decision to retire in 1993. "I felt like I needed a change. Bill had already retired. If I waited much longer, I wouldn't be able to find a new venue and have a real impact."

Beverly announced her plan to retire early in the school year to allow a smooth transition. She says now that she planned to do something else in education, although she didn't have a position lined up.

But others in Long Beach had a different idea. The city and state were in the midst of a recession. The Navy had announced that it would be closing the Long Beach Naval Station, taking with it the city's identity of the last 50 years.

Long Beach had only gone to a citywide elected mayor system six years before, when long-time City Council member Ernie Kell was elected for two years. He won a full term in 1990, and was seeking reelection in 1994. Two other experienced council members, Ray Grabinski and Jeff Kellogg, had plans to oppose Kell, as well.

Some wanted to see an end to politics as usual, though. And they had been watching Beverly's collaborative style of leadership work well at City College.

"I was retiring at the end of June," Beverly recalled. "Some time in April, someone came up and said they wanted to talk about me running for mayor. I laughed.

"Then in May, a group came again to ask me if I'd run. I said absolutely not. I wanted to finish being president the same way I started — absolutely committed."

Rather than dissuade her wooers, the statement confirmed what they had thought — Beverly's attitude was the type of leadership they were looking for. Among them was one of Beverly's friends and colleagues, Steve Horn. Horn had been president of California State University, Long Beach, when O'Neill was working on the seamless education initiative, and was in the midst of his own campaign for Congress.

"After I retired, Steve Horn came to talk," Beverly said. "He said I really should consider running. He said I could make a difference."

Saying that she could make a difference to the future of the city she loved was better than a dare to Beverly. It defined her mission. The city she had spent her entire life in, the city that had nurtured her and allowed her to succeed, needed her help.

That made Beverly's decision easy. She was in.

"When people first began talking to me about running for mayor, some would ask if I had fire in my belly," Beverly said. "I had no fire in the belly to be mayor, to be in politics. But I had a raging fire in my belly to make a difference. I became convinced I could make a difference as mayor."

CHAPTER **14**

The First Campaign

Beverly's commitment to the college, and her hesitance in jumping into politics, meant she would get a late start in her campaign. The group that wanted her to be their candidate waited until July. Then they brought in Democratic campaign consultant Don Foultz to offer advice.

"He said he would give me a month to do research," Beverly said. "But then he also said to hurry up and decide, so we could go after endorsements."

That research led to a number of discussions with city leaders. One of those talks was with Jay Oxford, general manager of the Long Beach Hilton in the 1990s, shortly after it was built.

"He said the hotel was not going to make it, that the city had to change or the hotel wasn't going to make it," Beverly recalled. "Downtown was a mess. We were going down the tubes. Our city was too good to allow that to happen... I think it was another opportunity to be in a position to give back to my community, to make a difference. I couldn't turn my back on that."

The decision was made; now a team had to be formed. That's where Beverly discovered just how strong a network she had forged in her years at City College. The list of potential supporters and helpers was long.

To balance the enthusiasm of volunteers, the O'Neill supporters brought in experienced political consultant Park Skelton to run the campaign. His advice to Beverly was to be herself — bright, prepared and above all, positive.

That positive approach set Beverly apart from the rest of the candidates. There were three long-time council members on the ballot, and all emphasized the financial crisis the city faced. Two newcomers, Frank Colonna and Don Westerland, had experience in business and also focused on the city's woes.

There was plenty to focus on. The Long Beach Naval Station was in the process of closing, the aircraft industry was in recession, Disney had been rebuffed in its efforts to create an ocean-side park and the city's downtown — like downtowns across the country — had lost its customer base. The state economy was in a recession and crime was on the rise.

Morale was low in the ranks of city employees. There was talk of disbanding the city's police department and turning to a contract with the Los Angeles County Sheriff's Department (as was the case in a number of surrounding cities). Although Long Beach was the fifth largest city in California and the 34th largest in the country, it seemed lost in the shadow of Los Angeles.

Beverly brought a different approach to the campaign. She unabashedly stated her love for her native city, and her belief that residents could make a positive difference if given the chance.

Beverly decided to be true to her non-politician self, and declined to run a political race. Pleas to offer fire and brimstone speeches were rebuffed.

"There's a big difference between campaigning and doing a job," Beverly says. "I was applying for a job. Some people who didn't understand that approach didn't think I could do the job."

Campaign stops included neighborhood groups, churches, service clubs and the like. Voters came up to Beverly with stories of singing with her in church choirs, knowing her through City College or working with her in the community. They could tell she was in it for the love of her city.

She was the only woman in the race. A political newcomer, she carried herself like a lady and was unfailingly polite, even to those who dismissed her candidacy as a whim of a well-liked but naïve community member. But those who dismissed her soon learned of their mistake.

Beverly's prominence in the city through her position at City College, her record of accomplishments and her spotless personal reputation made her an instant legitimate candidate. Her backers in the community gave her both credibility and sufficient resources to run a campaign.

Still, Beverly said the political arena seemed alien.

"I still remember the first debate, at Rogers Junior High," Beverly said. "I remember walking in thinking, 'What am I doing here?' We were like the evening's entertainment."

But she wouldn't be deterred, and she had long ago learned how to keep any uncertainty inside. And there were plenty of people on her side to help remind her to keep being herself.

Diane Jacobus met Beverly when a friend of a friend asked her to help with a fundraiser.

"It was in December 1993, and I agreed to do this thing with a cowboy theme," Jacobus said. "I did it, and I haven't been home since. After Beverly hired me full time, I just fell in love with her. I was totally committed. It was that way with everyone around her."

Jacobus would spend the next 13 years at Beverly's side. The connection was immediate, starting in the campaign.

"We seemed to just instinctively know what each other was thinking," Jacobus said. "To have Beverly O'Neill as a candidate was just incredible. She had been born and raised in the community. She had touched lives everywhere. I'd never worked in a campaign with so many volunteers."

"I remember one who was working the phone banks, Thelma Victoria. She kept saying 'Beverly Hills for mayor.' But the message came across."

The election results proved her point. Beverly finished well ahead of the pack in the city's April 1994 municipal primary. Councilman Ray Grabinski came in second.

After the primary, money and supporters poured in. The runoff election never seemed to be in doubt — it was a pre-inaugural procession. O'Neill won the office by more than 5,000 votes.

CHAPTER **15**

Madame Mayor

"I still don't feel like a politician," Beverly says today. "That's a dumb thing to say, because when you run, you're a politician. But winning doesn't make you smarter, richer or wiser. I believe you don't use the position, you don't think you are something special.

"For me, being a candidate was painful. There was sort of a sense of euphoria at the end, knowing we'd gone through a campaign and I felt my reputation was still intact."

In Long Beach, there is only a short transition period from election to taking office, especially when a runoff is required. The election is the second Tuesday in June; the swearing in is on the first Tuesday in July.

"We came in on the weekend to see the office," Jacobus said. "It was just us girls (including Cathy Wieder). She said we were going to kill them with kindness. There was a sense of fairness with everything she did from the very beginning."

Beverly and her staff worked primarily with City Manager James Hankla. Kell shut down his operation quickly, and returned to private life.

Hankla had met Beverly in her capacity as president of LBCC, and had been impressed. He says his first impression was verified when she became mayor.

"I was getting ready to leave (his position as city manager), but I wanted to work for her, so I stayed," Hankla said. "She was a student of everything, and she was a quick study. Above all, she listened."

Beverly's relentlessly positive approach prompted some to characterize her as a cheerleader. She did little to dissuade that notion when one of her first acts in office was to order "I 'heart' Long Beach" buttons.

It was more than cheerleading, though, Jacobus said.

"She wanted to share her love of the city," she said. "She wanted to share how good it had been to her. She believed people had to take pride in the city before they could make it better."

Beverly was using her bully pulpit as mayor to make people feel better about themselves, to convince them they could make a difference. She had to use the bully pulpit, because she had few other tools.

When Long Beach voted to create the office of a full-time, elected mayor, it was decided to limit that office's power by not allowing the mayor to vote on items before the City Council. Therefore, the mayor didn't have to take a position on every issue on the agenda. Beverly declined to make pronouncements in public, particularly during City Council meetings, in a desire to encourage open discussion among council members.

That, combined with the cheerleading aspect of Beverly's public persona, caused some to say she did not have an interest in policy. Nothing was further from the truth, Hankla said.

"She was an active participant when it came to formulating strategy, then she was able to be the front person for the strategy," he said. "She was like a partner. She didn't make you feel like you just worked here... and she never tried to be the city manager. She didn't want that."

Beverly adjusted quickly to her new position. Many facets of the job called on skills she had already developed.

"To be mayor wasn't as difficult as it was to be a candidate," she said. "It was similar to being president at the college, but on a much larger scale. Long Beach is unique in that we have our own health department, a port, an airport, our own water department, oil properties… The learning curve was straight up. Every day brought something new and different."

Sadly, not all those new and different things were good. Enter (or exit) the Navy.

CHAPTER **16**

The First Challenge

When Beverly took office in 1994, the decision had already been made to close the Long Beach Naval Station. The Naval Hospital, a 166-bed facility in the far eastern part of the city, closed in April, just before O'Neill took office.

The Naval Station was set to close in September 1994, reassigning 38 ships and 17,000 Navy personnel. In addition to the facilities at the Port of Long Beach, the Navy was giving up a large tract of Naval housing in west Long Beach.

More than the ships, the personnel and the economic underpinning were being taken. Since World War II, Long Beach had counted itself a Navy town. The very identity of the city was being taken away.

Beverly had learned, as early as in the AA days, that wallowing in self-pity solved nothing. Being busy, trying to improve one step at a time, countered the depression.

There was plenty to do. She rolled up her sleeves and started.

The city had created reuse plans for most of the parcels — expansion of the private shipping facilities at the Port of Long Beach where the Naval Station had been, a new big-box shopping center at the hospital site and a combination of research park, job corps center, new high school and a complex of services for the home-less at the sprawling Naval housing property. It was Beverly's job to see those plans to fruition.

The shopping center provided the first opportunity for diploma-cy. The city of Lakewood bordered the property and had to agree to the extensive highway improvements necessary to take advantage of the 605 Freeway running next to the proposed big-box center. But much of Lakewood's tax base came from sales at the Lakewood Mall just a few miles away, and leaders there could see little reason to cooperate with building a center to compete with their mall.

"We had already been warring with Lakewood for some time," Beverly said. "I called up their mayor and we sat down. We were able to agree that our cities needed to work together for the good of the region."

She makes it sound simple now, but the talks took most of a year. The result was a change in relationships between the cities from adversaries to partners.

And that good thing has been a boon for Long Beach, with the Towne Center rising to the point it is the second largest source of retail sales tax revenue in the city.

But even as Beverly and the city's staff worked to revitalize the property the city was vacating, they had to fight another battle. The Long Beach Naval Shipyard was on the next list of BRAC (Base Closure and Realignment Commission) closures.

Beverly and her first chief of staff, Randal Hernandez, mounted a full-court press to save the shipyard. They were joined by much of the city, including Ray Grabinski, O'Neill's most tenacious op-ponent in the '94 election. Her old ally, Steve Horn, did all he could as the lone Congressman from Long Beach.

"We knew the Navy was going to leave, that the station was going to leave," Beverly said. "But we felt the shipyard would stay. They told us to make it profitable, and we had. It was the most efficient shipyard on the West Coast, with the largest dry-dock available.

"We spoke at the BRAC hearing, and offered all our position papers. Everyone was wowed by what we had."

But what Long Beach didn't have was political and military clout. Horn was a lone voice in the capitol. Forces from San Diego lobbied long and hard to move the shipyard activities there. Not only was San Diego home to the Pacific Fleet, it was where many top Naval officers had retired. The efforts gained ground despite the fact that Long Beach had the only dry-dock on the West Coast large enough to handle a nuclear battleship.

"It all came down to politics," Beverly said. "San Diego had great say in what happened in the Navy. We really didn't have our day in court. And you know, San Diego never did build what they said they would build."

Beverly and her staff gathered to watch the final BRAC hearings. Wieder, who was then special assistant to the mayor and who would become chief of staff in 1999, remembers the moment 10 years later.

"It was really heart-breaking times," Wieder said. "Watching the BRAC hearing, we were really shocked. Beverly had been like a dog with a bone on the issue. No stone had been left unturned trying to save it.

"After the decision, it was like learning that someone had died. We were in mourning. Afterwards, she started looking for ways to overturn it. She was the ultimate fighter. She wouldn't give up until the day it closed."

Beverly said that the lowest point in her 12 years in office came facing the shipyard workers the day after the BRAC decision. She felt they had been let down, not by the effort put forth to save the shipyard, but by the decision to close it.

"The next step was taking care of the 5,000 people who were working there," she said. "I met with them the day after, and told them we had done everything we could to keep it from happening, but it wasn't enough. Then we had to move on."

During the reuse decision process, emphasis was put on efforts to find another shipbuilder for all or part of the facility. Beverly and the city staff wanted to save the skilled, high-paying jobs the shipyard represented. But none could be found with sufficient backing to keep the yard operating.

When it became clear that the private shipyard option wasn't viable, Beverly asked what the next highest economic use would be. The answer was expansion of the Port of Long Beach. Beverly fought to make the former shipyard part of the port's terminal operations. Despite opposition, she succeeded — and created jobs.

It is hard to find a better example of how Beverly's grounding in the world of Alcoholics Anonymous forged her approach to leadership than in how she dealt with the shipyard closure.

Think for a second about the Serenity Prayer, a staple of AA philosophy. It goes, "God, grant me the serenity to accept the things I cannot change, the courage to change the things I can, and the wisdom to know the difference."

Beverly fought the shipyard closure with all her energy — until it became clear it was something she could not change. Then she accepted that reality and began dealing with the things she could change — the city's attitude, the lack of an alternative approach and the paucity of resources. She had the courage to follow through on those opportunities to face the city's challenges. She changed the things she could.

CHAPTER 17

Time To Rebuild

Jerry Miller was manager of the city's Economic Development Bureau when Beverly became mayor. He had worked with her when she was at LBCC, where the city looked to train aerospace workers.

"That was when McDonnell Douglas (the airplane manufacturer) was going gangbusters," Miller said. "We formed a partnership to create an aerospace jobs center. They were coming in one door and going out another door to good-paying jobs. Then in just a couple of years, the world had changed. We were retraining people to go elsewhere.

"When Beverly became mayor, I took her on a tour of what we faced — losing the Navy, Boeing (which had purchased McDonnell Douglas) downsizing, the aftermath of the civil unrest in 1992… When she prepared her first state of the city speech, she came to us seeking things to highlight, but there wasn't much to offer."

Beverly remembers it another way.

"That first state of the city speech was the longest I ever gave," she said. "I spent 45 minutes trying to find anything possible that might be positive."

Loss of the Naval Station and its large population of direct and indirect jobs were estimated at a $1.8 billion annual hit to Long Beach's economy. Once the aerospace downsizing was included, the number of jobs lost topped 50,000. And these were high-paying manufacturing and government jobs.

The only bright spot, if there was one, was that the city had given the Navy some of the land its facilities were on. As part of the base reuse process, Long Beach had the first shot at offering plans to reuse the property — if they could convince the federal government that the uses made sense.

Beverly, the city management and the City Council knew that the top priority was rebuilding the city's financial base. It also had to create a new city image.

"We had been a Navy town for 60 years," Beverly said. "It was a bitter pill to realize you're losing your image as well as your economic engine and your tax base. We had to take a new direction."

Defying those who thought of her only as a cheerleader, Beverly offered a new vision for the city. She called it "The Three Ts and an R." It stood for Trade, Tourism, Technology and Retail.

Getting the City Council to follow her lead wasn't always easy, according to Jacobus. But Beverly flexed her facilitative leadership muscles.

"She accomplished what she wanted by convincing them to join the team," Jacobus said. "It was a true collaborative process, where they created a joint vision and went after it.

"I also have to credit Hankla for concurring with Beverly's approach. He backed her all the way."

It didn't hurt that Beverly's approach dove-tailed with what had already taken place in terms of planning the reuse of the Naval properties. The proposed Towne Center addressed her R of retail. The research park developed in conjunction with California State University, Long Beach, fit the T of technology, as did location of SeaLaunch on the Navy Mole in the Port of Long Beach. Creation of a new cargo terminal addressed the T for trade component.

The new Cabrillo High School, the Job Corps Center and the Villages at Cabrillo complex of homeless population services all provided badly needed public improvements.

SeaLaunch in particular was a coup for Long Beach. A partnership led by Boeing with companies from Russia, the Ukraine and Norway, it created a new, sea-based method of launching satellites into orbit — a highly technical endeavor. SeaLaunch began operations in 1995, launched its first satellite in 1999 and remains the largest private satellite launch operation in the world.

That left the T of tourism. Before Beverly took office, the city had tried hard to locate a new Disney by the Sea around the Queen Mary. That effort was foiled by the state Coastal Commission, which said an amusement park was not a proper use of waterfront property.

In fact, Beverly's predecessor, Ernie Kell, had counted on the Disney proposal as the city's savior. The entertainment company had taken over operation of the Queen Mary, but the city's icon quickly became an afterthought to Disney when the park proposal collapsed in the face of state Coastal Commission opposition. Kell's reliance on the failed project created a vacuum of planning that allowed O'Neill to lead a "revisioning" of the waterfront.

The City Council, with strong financial help from the Port of Long Beach, had also committed money to expand the smallish Convention Center to a size that would compete with San Diego and other comparable cities. But, aside from a medium-sized center called Shoreline Village, a Hyatt hotel next to the convention center and a downtown marina, the city's waterfront was essentially undeveloped.

The city hired Ehrenkrantz & Eckstut, a prestigious urban development planner, to come up with a master plan. The result was a proposal for a world-class aquarium, a public harbor for tall ships, dinner cruises and other attractions, and an entertainment-oriented retail area on both sides of Shoreline Drive, the waterfront street wrapping around the convention center. The basic concept came from the recently completed Baltimore waterfront development, which was being hailed as the most innovative in some time.

Early estimates of the cost of the public component of the development were $100 million. In a city that had just lost much of its tax base, the amount seemed insurmountable — except to a new, can-do mayor. Beverly was committed to the need to take advantage of the waterfront. It would be a step toward redeveloping all of downtown, as well.

"The entire city was hurting," she said. "We knew that. But I felt we had to change the downtown. We had to invest in the future, and the redevelopment of downtown was essential to that. The apple is only as strong as its core. It may be a cliché, but it's true."

So Beverly and the council decided to follow a dream. The next question was where the city could find the money to make the dream become reality.

Beverly had an answer.

"We knew that the most help would have to come from Washington," she said. "Our situation originated in Washington, so that's where we had to go."

CHAPTER 18

Mrs. O'Neill Goes to Washington

Beverly's first trip back to Washington, D.C., took place in late 1994. Democratic President Bill Clinton had taken office in 1992, and still had a Democratic majority. One of the first stops was the office of Attorney General Janet Reno.

"We were all sitting in the outer conference room, waiting for the attorney general," said Jerry Miller, who was with the group in his capacity as economic development officer. "Ms. Reno came out, and Beverly went right up to her. Reno invited her into her office and left us outside with some staff members.

"Pretty soon, we could hear laughter in there. We didn't know what it was about, and never found out, but when they came out, they were the best of friends. They were arm-in-arm, like sisters. That's just the way she (Beverly) worked."

Beverly said she and Reno had a lot in common. But it was a grant Long Beach didn't get that got her the one-on-one interview.

"I complimented her on the COPS (Community Oriented Policing Services) grants," Beverly said. "Then I asked her why we didn't get one, and suggested we might be good candidates the next year. That's when she invited me in to talk about it.

"Then we got to talking about our moms. We both had the same types of stories about our strong mothers. We connected."

That connection led to Reno visiting Long Beach the next year to review what was then a new student uniform policy at the Long Beach Unified School District — a visit that garnered national attention. Of course, Reno visited Beverly as well. Public safety was discussed.

And Long Beach received a COPS grant in 1995, the year after that first meeting.

Beverly made six trips back to the nation's capital before the end of 1996, all seeking support for Long Beach's resurrection. She says she was selling a vision and seeking partners to make that vision come true.

"We weren't just going back there and asking for money," Beverly said. "We had a plan. It's a cliché, but we weren't looking for a hand out, we were looking for a hand. We were willing to help ourselves. We just needed a little help to do it."

President Clinton's staff invited Beverly to bring a delegation to the capitol to state Long Beach's case. The group included then-CSULB President Robert Maxson, Harbor Commissioner Carmen Perez, banker Jim Gray (who Beverly had appointed the first chair of the Aquarium of the Pacific board), attorney Alan Tebbetts and council members Les Robbins, Mike Donelon, Alan Lowenthal and Jenny Oropeza (Lowenthal and Oropeza are Democratic stalwarts now in the California state senate). The group gathered to meet some of the top brass of the agencies the city hoped to do business with.

As was her normal mode of operation, Beverly had made preparations. With Miller in tow for technical support, she had gone to a Department of Housing and Urban Development conference in Florida specifically to meet Secretary Henry Cisneros. She knew that Perez, a force in the Democratic party in California, had a working relationship with Clinton's chief of staff, Leon Panetta, so she made sure Perez was part of the Washington trip.

"It was really up in the air as to whether the president would attend, though," Miller said. "That was the weekend of the Middle East peace talks. It certainly would have been understandable if he had bowed out.

"We were in the conference room, kind of tense. Carmen was talking with Mr. Panetta, as you would expect. Then we heard her say, 'Let's cut the crap, Leon. You know why we're here. We need money.' He just cracked up at that. It relaxed the atmosphere.

"Then the president came in. He went around the room, shaking hands with every single person there, including his own staff. Then he sat down at the head of the table, with Beverly to his right. Beverly said, 'Mr. President, congratulations on the peace accord,' and the room burst into applause. It was an amazing moment."

As is typical, Beverly downplays her role.

"The president presided at the meeting," Beverly recalls. "He walked in and shook hands all around. Then he stayed and allowed us to tell our story. That was something."

Beverly was well aware of how far she had come from the dark little apartment of her youth. She recalled another meeting with Clinton, this one with Democratic mayors, as one of the defining moments of her life.

"I was standing in the White House portico with Clinton and seven other Democratic mayors," she said. "I was looking out at the Washington Monument, not vice versa. I had to pinch myself to prove I was really on the inside of the White House."

Once Beverly began working to enlist Washington's assistance, she left no stone unturned. For example, the city's lobbyist gave her a heads-up that there would be a fundraiser for a Congressman in Monterrey, and that Panetta would be attending.

"Beverly led a delegation from Long Beach to the event," Miller said. "And she got her five minutes with Panetta."

Beverly also found common ground with John Emerson, Clinton's intergovernmental relations officer. Those relationships not only got Long Beach noticed at the White House, it gave entrée to the all-important department heads like Cisneros. Emerson helped navigate the maze of federal bureaucracy, as well.

"In terms of Queensway Bay (the name for the waterfront development), she made it happen," Miller said. "She got to know all the senior people in the administration... She went to a conference specifically to get next to Henry Cisneros, and got him to come out to Long Beach.

"We took him to the top of the Landmark Square building. Beverly started talking about Queensway Bay and her ideas with the Three Ts and economic development. It wasn't quite this simple, but by the time we came back down from the roof, we had the promise of a $40 million loan from HUD to do the infrastructure."

The strength of her impression on the country's leaders was strong. Clinton came out to Long Beach himself, to announce a contract for new Boeing C-17s but also to see for himself the many things Beverly had told him about.

Throughout her 12-year tenure, Beverly was able to go back to Washington to find support for her projects — although she admits it was more difficult after Clinton left office and Republican George W. Bush moved in to the White House. She said the reason she was so successful at lobbying the federal government was the city's ability to follow through.

"I remember going back one time for something and sitting outside the President's (Clinton's) office," Beverly said. "I heard someone, I think it was the President, say, 'they've never embarrassed us.' I took that as meaning we did what we said we were going to do with the money we received."

Clinton ultimately came to Long Beach three times while in office (once on a campaign trip) and came back in 2005 to speak before the Boys & Girls Club. Hillary Clinton, in another campaign stop, offered Beverly a high compliment for her work in Washington.

"I'm feeling a little insecure being on stage with Beverly O'Neill," Clinton said to the crowd. "Bill told me to say hello to his favorite mayor."

CHAPTER 19

On The Homefront

Beverly managed to forge the partnerships in Washington, D.C., by following her maxims of finding a vision and build a consensus around that vision amongst those who could make a difference. She used the same approach at home.

"She never used the word I," Jacobus said. "Everything we did was we. She talked to the employees all the time. Sometimes I think she was more comfortable with them than at appearances (in the public). Everyone loved her. How could they not?

"We had an attitude of 'just do it.' We thought we could do anything if we did it together."

Both Jacobus and Wieder use one word to describe their relationship with Beverly — love. It isn't typically a word associated with big city mayors, but it comes up often when those around her discuss Beverly.

"She has a presence," said Mike Murray, communications manager for Verizon and president of the Long Beach Chamber of Commerce during Beverly's time as mayor. "She draws people to her. You want to do the best you can for her. People love her."

The key, most agree, is Beverly's honest interest in the people around her. She learned to listen to — and care about — people from her parents and their relationship with people in AA. She took that approach to a high art.

"She gave me the opportunity to shine," Wieder said. "She had confidence in me, and let me know it… She was engaged in everyone's life, and it was genuine. You could tell. She'd bring back little trinkets for the staff, give out gift bags. We all believed in her, and would do anything for her."

Even after four years out of office, people approach her with thanks for coming to a public works employee breakfast or a non-profit group's lunch. She remains an "A list" invitation for any event, drawing large crowds at places as diverse as the Most Inspirational Student Dinner and a living history series at the Long Beach Historical Society.

There was a flaw in Beverly's approach, though, at least according to her. And the flaw, like the gift, came from her mother.

"I approached work with my mother's influence," she said. "She loved working with people. I have to admit, though, that sometimes for me the person became more important than the issue. That's not always good."

Many of the city's leaders begged to differ.

"Most politicians' accomplishments are measured with buildings, parks and initiatives," Murray said at O'Neill's retirement. "Other leaders go beyond structures and statistics. Their leadership overlaps into caring; touching souls and making people — all people — feel worthy. These are the leaders who inspire our hearts. Thank you, Mayor O'Neill, for giving us all a sense of worth."

Beverly would have plenty of buildings and statistics to boast about before she was finished. But she says to this day that making people feel a little better about themselves and their city is the thing she enjoyed doing the most.

"Sometimes I felt like a salesman telling the story of Long Beach," Beverly said. "The possibility was there, but it takes a while for everything to come together. I would tell people our story and invite them to capture the vision with me.

"People who were far-sighted would come with me. Because together, we could start seeing some change, some progress."

U.S. Sen. Diane Feinstein, who became a personal friend as well as a political ally, offers a slightly more effusive estimation of Beverly's impact.

"Beverly has been a major force in bringing together the community," Feinstein said. "She has helped Long Beach become a key economic player, both in the United States and throughout the world. She has helped her beloved city thrive through new advancements to infrastructure and by boosting Long Beach's economy with diversified trade, tourism and technology.

"Beverly has always shown that she was willing to do the hard work, and not only talks the talk, but walks the walk."

CHAPTER **20**

Building The Future

As is the case for most top leaders, one of Beverly's skills was surrounding herself with good people and allowing them to do what they did best. The Aquarium of the Pacific was a perfect example.

While the federal government could help with the infrastructure for the new waterfront, there was no way Washington was going to pay to build a $100 million aquarium. That would require a nonprofit board with enough clout to raise big bucks.

Beverly turned to a man who had made a fortune building an automobile dealership, and then built a new bank — Jim Gray. Gray had plenty of other irons in the civic fire, but he was one of the group that had convinced Beverly to run for mayor in the first place.

"I didn't go looking for this," Gray said of his chairmanship of the first aquarium board of trustees. "But when Beverly asks you to do something, well, you usually end up doing it."

Gray and the trustees took the Aquarium of the Pacific from an idea to a completely subscribed bond issue to opening day on June 20, 1998. It was no coincidence that Beverly began her second term as mayor just two weeks after that opening.

"By 1997, I just knew I had to run again," Beverly said. "There was just so much to do. We had the groundwork in place.

"There was no real opposition for the second term. It was wonderful — we could see the light at the end of the tunnel. We had the developers believing in us, the retailers were with us."

The national economy cooperated, and money was available for development as the end of the century neared. The big box Towne Center began construction in 1998 and, while there were delays in the retail component of the Queensway Bay as developer Oliver/MacMillan dickered for a better deal, Camden Development invested millions in the first new residential project downtown in years between the proposed Queensway Bay and Ocean Boulevard.

Beverly was working hard in Washington, concentrating on the trade portion of her three Ts. Although the Naval Station had closed in her first year in office, nothing had been allowed to replace it as 1998 began. Beverly said the politics was an eerie reminder of how the shipyard decision was made. She actually comes close to getting angry about how Long Beach had to relive the shipyard fight to be able to use the city's own land.

"The politicians in San Diego had great sway on what happened with the Navy," Beverly said. "Then we had Duncan Hunter and Duke Cunningham (Congressmen from San Diego) fight COSCO (China Ocean Shipping Company) as a tenant on the Navy land. So we had the 'Pinko' hearings."

COSCO had been a tenant in Long Beach for 17 years, sharing a terminal with another shipper. COSCO wanted to have its own state-of-the-art terminal, and the Naval Station property seemed to be the perfect opportunity.

Cunningham and Hunter argued that a company that was owned by the Chinese government would constitute a national security threat if allowed to have a container terminal in the Port of Long Beach. Beverly and Long Beach had no answer for the seemingly far-fetched scare tactic (this was four years before the

Sept. 11, 2001, terrorist attacks), and the deal was successfully blocked.

"There was no justification for their argument," Beverly said. "It was our land, and they were telling us what we could and couldn't do with it."

COSCO remained where it was. Due to the bitter debate, a companion firm, China Shipping Container Lines, turned its back on Long Beach and signed an agreement with the Port of Los Angeles as one of its major tenants, with a new terminal as part of the bargain. Ironically, COSCO and Chinese trade grew so rapidly that COSCO continues to lease space in Long Beach, and is one of the major customers. And Long Beach finally moved forward in 1998 with construction of a new shipping terminal on the largest portion of the Naval Station property.

"People really don't understand even today how big it was that we managed to use that property productively, to create jobs," Miller said. "It was because of Beverly's perseverance, almost completely. She knew how important it was."

At the same time, the long-awaited Alameda Corridor finally began construction. The corridor is a 20+ mile set of dedicated rail lines leading from the ports of Long Beach and Los Angeles to railyards near downtown Los Angeles. From those yards, cargo spreads out across the country.

"Bill Clinton laid the groundwork for that (the Alameda Corridor)," Beverly said. "Everyone thought that the largest port was New York and New Jersey. But the Atlantic Ocean was the older ocean, and we were the gateway to the Pacific. All of a sudden, we (Long Beach and Los Angeles) are the largest ports.

"With the trade sector growing, we could talk more about tourism."

That Alameda Corridor project also took one of Beverly's early city allies away. City Manager James Hankla decided to step down at the end of the year when offered the chance to head up the $2.4 billion construction project.

They continued to work together, though, and Hankla has taken on a number of projects for Beverly. After completing the Alameda Corridor construction, Hankla accepted an appointment to a six-year term as a Long Beach Harbor Commissioner at Beverly's request.

He remains impressed with her abilities.

"It was apparent early on that she was a special person," Hankla said. "That was true on a local, a state and a national level. It was almost as if she was ordained to be where she was.

"People can sense when a leader is letting self-interest rise to the top. That simply never happened with Beverly. Even those who disagreed with her couldn't say she wasn't doing what she thought was the best for Long Beach."

Hankla particularly stressed Beverly's ability to generate loyalty. As city manager, he had to be sure she knew about every employee recognition and gathering.

"She'd always show up to recognize the work of city employees and thank them," he said. "It means a lot. They'd feel valued, and they'd do anything for her."

What set Beverly apart was that she sincerely cared — she wasn't attending employee functions so the unions would later support her, or going to a small nonprofit's fundraiser in expectation of votes later. She wanted people to succeed, and she had learned in the AA years that she could help anyone succeed by providing support. So that's what she did.

But it wasn't all a lovefest for Beverly. The redevelopment of the Navy property, and particularly the downtown waterfront, brought out those who thought the city was going in the wrong direction. The most strident among them seemed to be against virtually everything the city, and Beverly, was trying to do. They became the CAVE people — Citizens Against Virtually Everything.

CHAPTER 21

How To Deal With Naysayers

As has been said before, one of the most basic traits of children of alcoholics is an aversion to conflict and confrontation. That tendency is in direct opposition to a career in politics or indeed any position of leadership.

Yet Beverly made it work. She did so by wearing her compassion on her sleeve, but knowing when to accept that she couldn't please everyone and moving ahead with her goals.

It was a learned skill.

"When I first became an administrator, I felt like a square peg in a round hole," she said. "I'd go into a faculty meeting, and want everyone to like me. The thing is, I really believe in people. Because of AA, I learned early to treat all people the way you would want to be treated."

As mayor, Beverly took that philosophy to a new level. Without exception, city employees talk first about how she cared about them, and then mention her policies or accomplishments.

The same philosophy played a major role in how she dealt with dissidents.

"She was unfailingly polite," her personal assistant, Diane Jacobus, said. "The council meetings sometimes were painful. I don't know how she did it. She would smile, listen and thank them for their thoughts."

Opposition is a constant for every city (or other) government around the world. For every person who thinks a project is a good idea, there seems to be at least one who thinks that project's implementation would be the worst thing in the world.

Beverly accepted, however reluctantly, that she wasn't going to convince everyone to get on board for every project. The trick, she said, was not taking it personally.

"You can't let the negative eat you up," she said. "You try to find a way to see what you can do about it, to unweave that hatred."

In Long Beach, the opposition centered around two factions. One group said that they were champions of the environment. After success in blocking a proposed sports park facility at the city's regional park, that loose affiliation coalesced into a strong anti-development voice involved in everything from use of the Naval Shipyard to the decision to use South American rain forest Ipe wood for the esplanade around Rainbow Harbor, where the Aquarium was located.

Another group seemed convinced that the city government was a vast conspiracy designed specifically to take everything from the "little people" and give it all to developers or themselves. These people consistently opposed all city policy, and coined the phrase "It's always the council's fault."

In many situations, the two groups joined forces. Using what then was an essentially new medium, the Internet, they kept pressure ratcheted up, and received far more attention than their numbers appeared to warrant.

Beverly unwittingly gave these opponents something to rally around. It happened in Chicago, at a meeting of the nation's mayors.

In a breakfast talk, Beverly mentioned a speech she had heard recently by a Texas mayor. In that speech, the mayor had talked about CAVE people — the folks in his town who were Citizens Against Virtually Everything.

A Long Beach reporter covering the mayor's convention asked about the acronym, the story hit the paper, and the group in Long Beach latched onto the label.

"The funny thing is, I never called anyone that," Beverly said.

Beverly remains sensitive to personal attacks, saying they have no place in debate of public policy (where she expects people to disagree at times). She seemed genuinely perplexed when she was subjected to personal attacks, Hankla said.

"Politics can be the most vicious arena in the world," Hankla said. "Beverly was unique in that world. In all my dealings with her, there was not a scintilla of self-interest. Her approach to the job was pure public service, and it was difficult to attack that."

CHAPTER 22

Changing Faces

While City Hall critics made noise, they had little concrete impact. When Beverly ran for her second term in 1998, no serious challenger surfaced, and she won more than 80% of the vote in the April primary election.

That vote was considered a mandate for the new direction Beverly, Hankla and the City Council had charted. At the same time, the real estate market boomed, filling both the city's and the Redevelopment Agency's coffers.

A large share of that government redevelopment effort was focused on the downtown portion of Long Beach. There was some assistance for redeveloping east Long Beach retail centers, and more to develop the City Center with its big box retailers including Sam's Club. Another coup, one that wouldn't really bear fruit until after Beverly's tenure, was the creation of the North Long Beach Redevelopment Project Area. The most impressive part of that effort was tying expansion of the Port of Long Beach to raising revenue for the redevelopment area.

But the big public money stayed downtown.

"We felt we had to change the downtown," Beverly said. "We had to invest in the future of the city, and the redevelopment of the downtown was essential to that.

"It's proven out. Now it is a major source of income. The next step is to build the residential areas, along with the residential services, so people will want to live there."

Those steps were in the future. Beverly appeared to be set to sail through her second — and apparently final — term, solidifying the partnerships and plans created in her first four years.

There were personnel changes to be dealt with. Hankla turned the bureaucratic reins over to his assistant, Henry Taboada. Beverly's chief of staff for the first four years, Randal Hernandez, decided to step down in April 1999, and Cathy Wieder was elevated to the top staff spot.

"She had more confidence in me than I had in myself," Wieder said. "When Randal told her (that he was leaving), that same day she told me I was going to be the new chief of staff.

"I knew right away I would follow her lead. Randal was superb at the inside game, the politics. It was tough going getting settled in — I'm not a micro-manager. It took some shifting around of responsibilities, but we put it together pretty quickly."

Taboada elevated Jerry Miller to the assistant city manager post, giving Beverly a strong ally in the city manager's office. While Taboada and Beverly respected each other and worked together, the relationship wasn't the same as it was with Hankla.

"Taboada had a different approach, a different management style," Jacobus observed. "They weren't as much of a team as it was with Hankla."

Perhaps more importantly, the ramifications of the 1992 passage of a two-term limit for the City Council and mayor began to be felt significantly in the same election that gave Beverly her second term. The seasoned council members she had forged partnerships with when she first was elected began to drop away.

The dean of council members, Tom Clark, had already stepped down in 1996 after 30 years of service. In 1998, Doug Drummond was termed out in the Third District and replaced by one of Beverly's former opponents, Frank Colonna. Les Robbins completed his second term in the Fifth District. Jackie Kell, the wife of the former mayor (who had held the Fifth District seat before the city began electing mayors citywide), jumped into politics to take the post.

And in a harbinger of what term limits would ultimately mean in California, Alan Lowenthal stepped down from the Second District seat after six years when he successfully ran for state Assembly. Dan Baker, the first openly gay City Councilman in Long Beach, replaced him.

With the change in council members came a shift in emphasis. For the most part, the previous councils had thought of the city as a whole first and their individual districts second. The new members focused more on their own district, where their voters resided. Beverly had to work harder to form the partnerships necessary to advance her vision of the city as a whole.

"I served with a total of 23 council members," Beverly said. "They were all different, all individuals, and I tried to treat them that way. They had different agendas, different priorities, but they all cared about the city… It was a matter of finding some consensus and moving forward."

Beverly's skills as a facilitative leader were tested in her second term, as she tried to lead an increasingly diverse and fractured team of political leaders. She succeeded behind the scenes by finding common ground — and building on it.

CHAPTER 23

A Perfect Fit

In many ways, Long Beach's mayor's position was structured so only someone like Beverly could be successful. When she was first elected in 1996, the city had had a full-time, citywide popularly elected mayor for only six years.

Perhaps in reaction to the strong mayoral form of government in neighboring Los Angeles, the people who structured the full-time mayor's post to put before a vote of the people left the position largely powerless — much like the ceremonial mayor chosen from amongst the nine council members before 1988. In fact, as a council person, that ceremonial mayor had one thing the new full-time mayor didn't — a vote.

A mayor, much like a governor or a president, isn't meant to be part of the legislative branch of government, so it made sense that a citywide mayor wouldn't have the same vote a mayor chosen from among peers would enjoy. But those who decided to change the Charter apparently couldn't convince themselves or the electorate to create a true executive branch, either.

In 1996, Long Beach's mayor had no real veto power — a veto on everything but the budget could be overturned by a simple majority. The city manager had the responsibility for creating the annual budget, with the mayor allowed only to offer potential ad-justments — and the council had the final vote on the spending plan. (Beverly did threaten once to veto a budget proposal, but did not have to follow through on the threat.)

Neither the mayor, nor the City Council, had control over per-sonnel hiring and firing decisions except for two posts — the city manager and the city clerk. The city manager even hired the po-lice chief and the fire chief, although the council typically vetted the choice.

So how did Beverly become known as one of the nation's most effective leaders?

Edward Herbert Ogle completed his doctoral dissertation in 2000. His topic was Beverly's leadership style — he called it transformational leadership, but defined it in a way similar to Beverly's definition of facilitative leadership.

"Beverly's ingredients for success ... along with an agenda that includes setting the atmosphere, setting the tone, believing in the process and communicating that belief to others, explains Beverly's long and successful tenure as a transformational leader," Ogle writes. "One of the identifying characteristics of a transfor-mational leader is that the leader is not subject to environmental circumstances but (is) more effective in creating and, therefore, shaping the milieu."

For Beverly, that environment was relentlessly positive. She saw the good and pointed it out. She seized on the things that could be changed and set out to change them. And she convinced oth-ers that they were more effective working together than they were working separately.

"In my definition, it was a matter of facilitating a shared vi-sion," Beverly said. "I strived to inspire others to commit their en-ergy to a common purpose.

"People support what they help to create. I don't care who gets the credit, and I've discovered that none of us is as smart as all of us."

That also was the way she inspired the people around her —
in particular, the city's employees. While the public saw her at
virtually every event around the city, employees also saw her at
their own gatherings, or while they were on the job.

"At events, she might be there to cut the ribbon, but she also
was there to cheer on staff," Jacobus said. "She would always
respect and uplift the invisible people, the workers who made it
all happen. She'd never miss a Public Works breakfast. She would
talk to employees all the time — I think she was more comfortable
with them.

"Everyone loved her. It's not a word you associate often with a
mayor, but it's true. She had an attitude of just do it, and we knew
there was nothing we couldn't do with her behind us."

Beverly's secret was an honest concern with those around her.
She was an active listener and people responded to that. That
worked for the community as well as the city's employees.

"We'd go to three, four, sometimes five events," said Mike
Sanders, Beverly's speechwriter and assistant. Sanders, Wieder
and Jacobus shared the job of keeping up with the super-active
mayor. "She knew what it meant to people that she was there, and
hated to say no. It was tough to keep on time, too, because she'd
always stop and talk. She wanted people to know she appreciated
what they did for the city."

Again, Beverly's approach can be traced back to her experiences with Alcoholics Anonymous through her parents. She
learned early on how to listen and be supportive. The basic tenet
of facilitative or collaborative leadership— the group is stronger
than the individual — comes straight from AA's reliance on the
group assisting and supporting the individual in the effort to overcome alcohol.

In AA, small victories add up to big successes. (How do you get
a month of sobriety? One day at a time. How do you get a year of
sobriety? One day at a time.) Beverly helped everyone around her
have small victories. She, and the city, had some big successes.

CHAPTER 24

Openly Optimistic

"Serving with Mayor O'Neill at a critical time in the city's history was a great privilege and a totally positive experience," James Hankla said. "It was probably as close to Camelot as a city manager ever gets."

Hankla had moved on to the Alameda Corridor by 1999, but Long Beach at that time under Beverly did seem to be on the verge of a Camelot-like renaissance. Beverly's vision — a revitalized urban core enhanced by a destination waterfront, a burgeoning trade sector generating jobs, technology-driven booms in education and industry, all enhanced by increasing retail opportunities across the city — was moving ahead full-steam.

A booming national economy was cooperating, and the Clinton administration was making sure its commitments were completed before the end of Bill Clinton's tenure. With the necessary government support in place, it was time for private developers to step up.

Convincing those naturally skeptical investors is where Beverly excelled. She would return to the skills of straight-forward explanation and active listening that she had learned those long years ago with Flossie and the ever-skeptical alcoholics they served.

While Beverly was comfortable in front of crowds, she was at her best one-on-one or in small groups. That's where her facilitative skills could be used to best advantage, Wieder said.

"She had a vision, and she relied on Hankla, Miller and the rest of us to put it together," Wieder said. "She would come into a room and facilitate the discussion. She would articulate the vision, and she would express confidence in the experts that they would come up with the details."

Miller said the ease with which Beverly advanced an agenda was the product of hard work and preparation.

"She wasn't a micro-manager, but she was always prepared," Miller said. "She knew where she wanted to go, and she knew who and what she needed to get there. But she would let the people in the room come to the conclusion that they wanted to go where she wanted to go."

Those details ranged from ways to use tax incentives to spur development to support for innovative mixed use approaches combining new retail with new housing. A very physical manifestation of changing the old for the new took place downtown with the demolition of the enclosed Long Beach Plaza shopping mall in exchange for the new CityPlace, which emphasized an open, outdoor feel for stores coupled with upscale apartments and condos either upstairs or in the same area.

A parallel move managed to maintain some of the character of historic downtown Long Beach, again with a nudge from Beverly and a big push from redevelopment resources. Historic buildings were converted, in whole or in part, to loft apartments and condominiums, drawing premium prices while maintaining historic facades. Add more modest artist live-work spaces in and around the East Village, and the housing choices multiplied.

It was the beginning of a residential boom that had more than 5,000 units either built or on the drawing board before the end of Beverly's tenure.

The list of city accomplishments in 1999 and 2000 reads

like a flow chart emanating from Beverly's "Three Ts and an R" vision.

Epson America moves its headquarters to Long Beach in 1999 (technology). The Long Beach Performing Arts Center and Center Theater restoration is completed in 1999 (tourism). United Parcel Service (UPS) opens its LB Gateway in 1999 (trade). The Towne Center big box stores and complementary 26-screen movie theater open in 1999 as the biggest retail center in the region (retail).

Sea Launch completed its first successful satellite launch in 1999 and moved its world headquarters to Long Beach in 2000 (technology and trade). The Wrigley Marketplace opened in 1999 and the Trader Joe's opened in Bixby Knolls in 2000 (retail). The Lions Lighthouse for Sight lit up in Rainbow Harbor in 2000, and the Long Beach Museum of Art opened a new gallery building the same year (tourism). Construction began on the new Emergency Communications and Operations Center (technology). The list goes on.

But Beverly's emphasis on getting Long Beach back on its financial feet wasn't her only interest. Beverly always had time for education efforts. She helped campaign for the passage of Measure A, the first K-12 school construction and renovation bond issue approved in 20 years, and lent her support two years later to a bond issue for LBCC, as well.

And while Beverly left performing behind early in her education career, she never lost her belief that the arts and humanities are a path to the soul.

That belief surfaced even as she negotiated with national leaders. She easily mixed talks of Naval Station reuse with musings about the potential for a Smithsonian Institution presence in Long Beach.

In partnership with Sandra Gibson, then-executive director of the Public Corporation for the Arts in Long Beach, Beverly made those dreams become reality in 1999. Very high building and security costs, as well as the political reality that was Washington,

D.C.'s possession of the nation's museum, made it unrealistic to consider opening a "Smithsonian West" year-round physical presence. But Long Beach did become the first municipality in the country to have a formal affiliation with the nation's museum.

"Of course I wanted Lincoln's hat," Beverly said at the time. "But this is the next best thing. It allows us to tap into the incredible knowledge and talent of the Smithsonian."

In a touch of showmanship, the Smithsonian secretary (equivalent to the executive director) at the time, Lawrence M. Small, came to Long Beach to formalize the affiliation and presented Beverly with Lincoln's hat. Or rather, the replica of Lincoln's hat sold in the Smithsonian gift shop. Only then did he and the mayor sign the affiliation agreement.

The partnership led to 10 years of programs with Smithsonian scholars interacting with Long Beach children and adults. Literally thousands of school children were touched by what Beverly began by musing about a hat.

For Beverly, the performing arts had been one of the few joys in her early life. When she was singing, she was in a world of pleasure instead of pain. She found solace in church music, and the fact she says even today that her biggest triumph in high school was winning the lead in "The Mikado" shows in what high esteem she held the arts.

At Long Beach City College, Beverly nurtured the theater arts program in particular. One of her professors, Shashin Desai, was an ambitious young Indian director with a vision for a professional theater in Long Beach.

In 1985, Beverly paved the way for Desai at City College when he launched International City Theatre, a professional troupe designed to complement the student productions at LBCC. The talent pool was certainly available — Long Beach is 20 minutes away from Hollywood.

As usual, Beverly found a way to sell a good idea to the powers that be. She convinced her trustees that students would benefit by working with professionals. The opportunity would draw more talented students, enhancing City College's programs.

It worked. By the mid-1990s, Desai had established a regional reputation for high-quality theater, particularly with dramas. He had outgrown the small black-box theater on the LBCC campus, and was hungry for more.

Who else would he turn to if not to Beverly? Now mayor, she was interested in creating more of an artistic critical mass, and Shashin was in search of a "real" theater.

So International City Theatre headed downtown, to the Center Theater, The smaller performance space had been part of the grand Performing Arts Center built as part of the Convention Center, providing an alternative to the 1,900-seat, three-level Terrace Theater where the Long Beach Symphony performed.

Beverly never took credit for moving ICT downtown, although she did step onto the stage in a cameo role during Desai's first production at the Center Theater in 1997. She also supported naming ICT the resident theater company for the Center in 1999, and it was her idea to label the Terrace-Center theaters complex the Long Beach Performing Arts Center, and brand it with a lighted sign that could be seen blocks away down Long Beach Boulevard.

"When I proposed a program to bring professional actors to the campus, Beverly was very, very helpful," Desai said when Beverly retired as mayor. "She not only encouraged me, but became a founding member informally, writing letters, helping with planning.

"Any time we needed her to appear at an event or an opening, she was there. I hold her very dear to my heart."

Not every effort to support the arts was as successful. Beverly went to bat early in her first term for the Long Beach Civic Light Opera, a group mounting large musical theater productions at the Terrace Theater, when they found themselves in dire financial straits. She convinced the City Council to provide a $1 million loan, guaranteed by revenue from the center's parking garage.

Less than two years later, the Civic Light Opera declared bankruptcy and closed its doors. The city eventually got its money back, but the experience had Beverly seeking a dedicated source of revenue to support the arts for the rest of her time as mayor.

Her unwavering support for the arts earned her many awards and unending loyalty and love from the city's arts community. To this day, any artistic soiree is incomplete unless Beverly is there to lend her smile. It may have been a result of reality in recession-ravaged 2009, but in the arts community, Beverly's tenure already is known as the good old days.

She wasn't shy about using good fortune to help the less fortunate, either. Part of the Naval land reuse package deal was creation of services for the homeless. Long Beach, with Beverly's insistence, created a Multi-Service Center in 1999 offering "one-stop" shopping for homeless people and followed that in 2000 with the Villages at Cabrillo, a center where several agencies offer everything from housing to job training.

She spent countless hours helping charities around the city, both by appearing at events and by working to convince others to support good causes. The Long Beach Day Nursery flourished under her patronage, as did the Flossie Lewis Center, but Beverly spread her support as far as it would go. The vast majority of those four or five events a night she attended were nonprofit functions that drew crowds based at least partially on Beverly's presence.

It is an old AA adage, or rather a basic AA tenet, that you will get better yourself by helping others get better. Beverly wasn't looking to get better herself, but she was looking to help her city get better.

Another old adage urges you to make hay while the sun shines. Beverly and Long Beach did just that as the 20th Century came to an end. But there were clouds on the horizon.

CHAPTER 25

Storm Clouds Gather

While there were plenty of triumphs for Beverly and the city as the 20th Century came to a close, there were signs of difficulty, as well. A key problem was the continued delay of the Pike at Rainbow Harbor retail development, which was supposed to create the critical mass of attractions required to create a regional destination.

But developer Oliver/McMillan struggled to lease spaces in the proposed development, and returned to the city more than once for additional changes and concessions in their development agreement. The council issued ultimatums; the developer threatened lawsuits. With no construction in sight in 2000, the Aquarium of the Pacific began struggling, and ultimately had to refinance their construction bonds.

Of longer lasting impact was the successful initiative in November 2000 to cut the city's Utility Users Tax in half, from 10% to 5%. The move chopped several million dollars from the city's general fund revenue, but perhaps more importantly appeared to signal the first crack in support for Beverly's vision of the city's future.

Beverly responded to the adversity as she always had — by

being positive. While the Pike languished, she supported creation of Cesar Chavez Park, the first new large park in the city in two decades — and in the middle of downtown where it was needed most. She worked even harder on her Three Ts and an R approach to increasing the city's tax base.

Some political observers began shaking their heads when some of the council members banded together to oppose a second term as a Harbor Commissioner for George Murchison. Murchison was a friend of Beverly's, and had been a pillar of the nonprofit and education communities for years.

"Beverly was upset by what they did to George," Jacobus recalled. "They wanted to make a point, and they took it out on a good man."

Beverly never appreciated it when people made politics personal and hurtful. But instead of taking the fight public, Beverly chose another strong supporter — one she knew the council could not find fault with — John Calhoun.

Calhoun had recently retired after a long career as City Attorney (an elected position in Long Beach charged with acting as the city's, and the City Council's, attorney). His office also represented the port, but did so with an assistant attorney dedicated specifically to the port. Calhoun had taken the city's point of view to the virtually autonomous Harbor Commission on many occasions. He was confirmed unanimously — and became a strong voice for the port in the next six years even while maintaining an understanding of the city's needs.

Beverly's other appointments to the same commission showed a true finesse in terms of facilitating a more harmonious relationship between the City Council and the Harbor Commission. She tapped one of the old guard from the council, Doris Topsy-Elvord, after Topsy-Elvord had been termed out of her council seat. The appointment worked in a number of ways. As a council member, Topsy-Elvord represented the inner city and the African-American population — the workers instead of the captains of industry. Yet

Topsy-Elvord understood how the port functioned as the city's primary economic engine.

But Beverly saved her best for last. Her final appointment to the Harbor Commission was none other than James Hankla. No council member dared question Hankla's commitment to the betterment of the city as a whole — he was, after all, the city manager who first convinced the port to start transferring 10% of its net profits to the city's Tidelands Fund, and shepherded agreements that had the port help pay for the convention center expansion, creation of the World Trade Center and more.

Once at the port, Hankla led the charge to make the Port of Long Beach the most ecologically-sensitive port in the world. At the same time, he maintained the business approach that allowed the Trade T in Beverly's Three Ts and an R to remain strong. The partnership that marked the beginning of Beverly's tenure lasted until the end of her stay at that post, and the friendship continues today.

Another crisis generated by outside forces threatened to leave an entire section of the city without easily accessible emergency health care. Catholic Healthcare West, which operated St. Mary Medical Center downtown, had purchased the eastside Long Beach Community Hospital in 1998, and then attempted to keep both hospitals viable through consolidation of administrative and other services. But the effort failed, and CHW decided to close Community Hospital.

The action left east Long Beach without a hospital, and perhaps more importantly, an emergency room.

Because the city had originally donated the land to build the hospital some 70 years before, it had a claim. The deed said the owner had to operate a hospital there, or return the property. Beverly, along with support from the City Council and particularly the council members from east Long Beach, facilitated the negotiations to have CHW deed the land and the buildings back to city ownership, along with several million dollars worth of equipment.

She then lent her support when a local group of doctors and residents formed a group to take the operation over and reopen the hospital.

Community Hospital closed its doors in September 2000. In a rare example of bureaucratic speed helped along by political will and community support, a deal was struck, $20 million raised and the hospital reopened in just nine months. It was then, and remains today, a much smaller operation than the one CHW closed, but it also stands almost alone as a hospital reopened in an era of hospital closures.

In this case, as was the case throughout her tenure, Beverly worked behind the scenes to gain consensus and buy-in. She gave credit for the political will to the two impacted council members, Frank Colonna and Dennis Carroll. She publicly praised Deputy City Manager Chris Davis for her diligence and privately helped move obstacles from Davis's path. When it came to private fundraising, no one would say as much, but the list of hospital donors bore a more than passing resemblance to Beverly's campaign list.

In other words, she facilitated. And her trademark smile was larger than ever the day the ribbon was cut to reopen the reborn Community Hospital of Long Beach.

President Bill Clinton opens a meeting between Long Beach representatives, cabinet members and staff. Beverly is at extreme right, Councilman Les Robbins and Harbor Commissioner Carmen Perez sit on the right side of the table. Clinton staff members are on the left.

Beverly and Jim Gray watch election results in her first reelection campaign.

Beverly greets Prime Minister Margaret Thatcher.

Beverly greets Transportation Secretary Norman Mineta.

Beverly and family at the 1994 Belmont Shore Christmas Parade.

Beverly and President Bill Clinton share a personal moment.

CHAPTER **26**

Leadership in Crisis

As the 20th Century came to an end, Long Beach moved forward with its recovery — sometimes seemingly despite itself. Beverly maintained a positive focus in public, but was beginning to run up against a more recalcitrant City Council.

"The first councils had a quicker understanding of the city as a whole," she said. "They understood that when the city as a whole benefited, their constituents benefited. The people after that had more of a 'my district first' attitude, and they questioned more. But we still advanced as a city. We had caught on."

Just getting out of the 20th Century and into the 21st was a bit of a struggle. The entire country was concerned about Y2K, in particular how the change from 1999 to 2000 would impact computers. Plenty of preparation made the computer switch take place smoothly, but the worries about some end-of-century calamity kept people home, cancelled a New Year's Eve bash downtown and severely cut attendance at other events.

Late in 2000, Beverly and Long Beach lost major allies when the Democrats and Bill Clinton's vice president, Al Gore, lost the White House to Republican George W. Bush.

More was in play than the difference in political parties, though.

There was an attitudinal difference as well — one that Beverly reflected on after watching eight years of the Bush administration.

"Bill Clinton came to the White House a governor (of Arkansas)," Beverly said. "I think he left as a mayor (understanding the issues facing cities). George Bush came to the White House a governor (of Texas) too, but I think he left as a governor (not embracing the needs of cities, perhaps because of a focus on national security)."

Fortunately, most of the financial rebuilding support for Long Beach was in place before President Clinton left office. Beverly maintained plenty of contacts and clout in Washington, D.C., and she would have entrée to the Bush White House, but the level of personal relationship wasn't the same.

Even with the shift in national administration, Long Beach moved ahead as 2001 became reality. Despite some fits and starts in terms of developers, Beverly's vision continued to take shape.

Then came Sept. 11, 2001, the day that changed America. Nearly 3,000 people died in the terrorist attacks that destroyed the Twin Towers in New York City, and the very heart of the nation's military defense, The Pentagon, was successfully attacked. The death toll was larger than that in the attack on Pearl Harbor.

Even while the nation mourned, its leaders mobilized to make sure there were no more attacks. While the use of commercial airplanes for the attacks put much of the focus on airport security, it was clear identification of potential targets was also a priority if another disaster was to be diverted.

Aside from the shock factor, it was decided that the Twin Towers had been attacked in large part because their destruction would seriously impact the country's economy (as it did). Using that rationale, it seemed clear that the Port of Long Beach combined with the Port of Los Angeles would make a very attractive target for terrorists.

A weeks-long strike in 1999 by longshoremen had crippled trade and retail operations in the entire western half of the country, showing just how significant an impact shutting down the ports could have. Add the hundreds of thousands of people living within "blast range" of the ports, and anxiety was high.

As mayor, Beverly saw her role as two-fold. She had to convince the residents that the city was doing everything necessary to keep them safe. She also had to make sure that everything really was being done.

"We had to show that we still were in control," she said. "We had to remain calm and deal with the situations as they arose. We let our people know we were doing everything we could to make them safe."

Beverly clearly reached back to her experience with AA here, as she took a bad situation and made the best of it. She didn't sit and moan about the situation, she did what she could to improve it, and left the rest to a higher power.

In addition to the calm demeanor of a leader she showed to the public, Beverly went to work behind the scenes. Because the Sept. 11 strike dealt with airplanes, the emphasis for Congress — once they decided to start spending money on security — was on stopping more terrorists from getting on airplanes. That meant the ports had to be satisfied with the leftovers.

At least that was the case the first year. Beverly quickly became an expert in port security — in fact, "the" expert when it came to elected officials. She went to California's senators, Diane Feinstein and Barbara Boxer, armed with both an explanation of the need and a list of the resources required to meet that need. Congresswoman Juanita Millender McDonald also proved to be an important ally.

"We raised awareness of the ports as the largest in the country," Beverly said. "I became versed in oceanfront security because I had to become an expert to do my job. We worked closely with the Coast Guard.

"We were fortunate to have a regional approach. We have a dense population, and a strong emergency response community. We were able to build and strengthen coalitions in the process."

Some argue the ports still don't have the support they need for adequate security. But the fact is, there are container scanners, a joint security center, a video surveillance system and more, largely thanks to the leadership of Beverly O'Neill. She showed there was a need, and a plan to fulfill that need, then went out and got the help needed to get the job done.

CHAPTER **27**

Decision Time

Despite all the efforts to alleviate the impacts of the terrorist attacks, the economy went into a tailspin, both nationally and locally. Hit particularly hard were the tourism and convention businesses that Beverly and the city had worked so hard to build. People were afraid to travel, and both family vacations and company conventions were canceled.

That meant fewer retail tax dollars and a drop in the city's bed tax revenue. The multiplier — waitresses made fewer tips, cooks and housekeepers got fewer hours, etc. — caused the city's tax revenue to shrink even more.

Before the federal government stepped up with financial aid to help pay for terrorist counter-measures, the city spent hundreds of thousands of dollars it hadn't budgeted on heightened security. Everything from the airport to the city's water supply required more manpower and technology to be sure they were safe.

At the same time, the reduction of the Utility Users Tax began to make a serious impact on the city's budget. The combination of factors uncovered once again a structural deficit that had been warned of in the mid-1990s, but had been covered in 1998-2001 with a booming economy.

"There were budget problems pretty much all along when I was mayor," Beverly said. "There was a glimmer of hope around 1998, but we spent it all in those few years… But you can't let the negatives eat you up. You find a way to see what you can do about it."

In 2001, Community Hospital of Long Beach reopened, and Carnival Cruise Lines brought the cruise ship industry to Long Beach with a terminal next to the Queen Mary (using part of the Spruce Goose Geodesic Dome to do it). But the economic uncertainty had slowed both retail and residential development. The lack of progress on the Pike at Rainbow Harbor project left a glaring hole in the city's vision of a new waterfront.

Beverly entered what appeared to be her last year as mayor, beginning on July 1, 2001, with unabated popularity. Due to the term limit law, she could not appear on another mayoral ballot. From the public's point of view, she was poised to end eight years in office with a victory lap.

But the public's view wasn't necessarily Beverly's view.

"I was thinking that if I could run for two more years, it would be perfect," Beverly said. "We had been able to get the infrastructure in, but it wasn't finished… I wasn't going to let years of planning go down the drain."

Beverly put out a few feelers to find out how people might respond to a write-in campaign for a third term. As the term-limit law was written, not only was Beverly banned from appearing on the primary ballot, she also could not appear on the run-off ballot should she make it that far.

"We truly felt that we hadn't completed what we wanted to do," Cathy Wieder said. "With her work ethic, we just knew we weren't going to leave things undone. There was no doubt in our mind we were going (for a third term)."

Many of Beverly's friends and supporters were leery. After an outstanding run, they wanted to see her go out on top. If anything, a run for state or national office seemed in order.

But Beverly wasn't concerned about her reputation, her career or her legacy. She was concerned about her city. And she was positive she still could make a difference.

"I sat down with Park Skelton (the campaign consultant who had run her first campaign)," Beverly said. "He counseled me. He said, 'The people know you. It's a matter of showing them how to vote.' I didn't know it had never happened before (election of a major city's mayor as a write-in candidate), but I really did want to see that waterfront finished."

The die was cast. In spring 2001, a year before the primary election, O'Neill announced — with a box of pencils in hand — that she was running for a third term as Long Beach's mayor.

Plenty of people had tried to talk her out of the run — including both of the major newspapers in town. But no one doubted that she had plenty of what the second verse of the Serenity Prayer calls for: "The courage to change the things I can." Now it was time to find out if she had the third part of that plea — "the wisdom to know the difference."

In the previous four years, one of Beverly's strongest allies was Third District Councilman Frank Colonna — the same businessman who had started his political career with a strong showing in the 1994 mayoral race. Colonna had indicated he was preparing another run for mayor, but announced he would defer to Beverly just days after her announcement.

Another of Beverly's 1994 opponents, Ray Grabinski, had other ideas. Grabinski had returned for one final term as a councilman in 1998, and then decided his only hope to continue a political career was as mayor.

Norm Ryan, the man behind the Utility Users Tax cut initiative, ran for the Third District council seat in 1998, but finished a distant third. With Colonna back for a second term there, Ryan decided to try his luck against Beverly.

But Beverly's strongest opposition would be a relative newcomer — Second District Councilman Dan Baker. Baker had won a special election for the council seat in 1999, then a full term in 2000, as the first openly gay council member in Long Beach. A young, charismatic candidate, Baker argued that the city wanted change and he would be the agent for that change, and with the established credentials Ryan couldn't claim. Baker didn't shy away from suggesting that Beverly's generation needed to step aside and allow new leadership to take over.

Beverly's approach was to stay the course and complete what the city had begun. She remained convinced that Long Beach had a positive future, and that the majority of the city's residents agreed with her. They just needed a little convincing.

For Beverly and her staff, the election strategy came down to teaching her core supporters how to mark ballots for a valid write-in vote. They knew they had a good core of support.

"The first poll showed that we didn't have the numbers," Diane Jacobus said. "But no one could catch up with what Beverly had. We were never on the ballot, but we never lost the lead."

Beverly deliberately began the campaign early to allow time to educate the voters. But it also meant that she had to run her office and the city for a year while campaigning at the same time.

Beverly was careful not to blur the line between the political campaign and the day-to-day business of her office. Wieder, for example, stayed away from all of the political events, concentrating on business.

That didn't make it easy, though. Two current council members were running against Beverly, and others were running for re-election in their own right.

"Things were pretty tense on the 14th floor," Wieder said. "Especially with the Baker office. But once the primary was over, things relaxed a bit."

That primary took place on April 9. About 42% of the votes were turned in before that day as absentee ballots — an emphasis for Beverly because it was simpler to explain how to mark the ballots to a person taking the time to read than to someone walking into a voting booth.

Baker had raised more money than Beverly, and had won the endorsement of the powerful Police Officers Association (Beverly countered with an endorsement from the Firefighters Union). But Baker was caught up in controversy over a negative campaign mailer against Grabinski, while Beverly kept her campaign focused on the positive.

The result was a win for Beverly. She finished ahead of the pack. Baker finished second.

According to the city Charter, only the top two finishers move on to the runoff election. But there had never been a write-in candidate in a Long Beach primary, let alone a write-in candidate who had won a spot in the runoff election. Ryan took advantage of that, and filed to be allowed to run in the final election as a write-in alongside Beverly. He was successful, while Beverly supporters lost a bid to have her name appear on the ballot (a law that has since changed).

The result was a final election ballot with only Dan Baker's name appearing. But by now, Beverly's positive approach clearly resonated with the voters, and the difficulty of casting a write-in ballot appeared to have been overcome. Still, Beverly never took anything for granted.

"The only thing Baker had to worry about was a maybe a hanging chad," she said. "Our voters had to take four steps to make their vote count. I still can't believe so many people did that."

That "so many" was about 47% of all the voters for Beverly. It gave her an easy victory, with nearly 3,000 more votes than Baker. Ryan only garnered about 16% of the total, but that did manage to create the unusual result of a runoff winner with less than 50% of the total vote. Still, it was a clear victory.

It was a victory won by personal contact, too. Beverly seemed to pick up energy as the campaign progressed, and continued to use her strength — listening to and talking to people.

"I just ran across someone the other day I met during that campaign," Beverly said. "She was one of the toothpick ladies at Costco — you know, the people handing out samples. I had stopped for a sample and talked to her for a bit (during the campaign). When I saw her the other day, she said that ever since she had been telling everyone she had lunch with the mayor. I loved that."

What Beverly and her campaign had accomplished was historic. No other big-city mayor in the country had ever been elected as a write-in candidate once, let alone twice, without being on the ballot.

"We had the (U.S.) Conference of Mayors convention right after the election," Wieder said. "She was literally a rock star. Her name was all over the place. I think they're still talking about it."

True to form, Beverly credited her supporters for the victory. But it was clear that it took a positive presence to galvanize those supporters, and Beverly fit the bill.

More important, she had remained positive throughout the campaign, never offering a negative word about any of her opponents. She counted on her passion for the city to come through. Just as with her first campaign, she could say she had come through the election with her reputation for fairness and positive campaigning intact.

CHAPTER 28

Expanding Horizons

Beverly had already established herself nationally, chairing committees on education and jobs for the U.S. Conference of Mayors. But her write-in victory made her a celebrity. True to form, she used the attention to further enhance Long Beach's stature.

Once her third term had been assured, Beverly was elected to the U.S. Conference's executive committee, putting her on a path to become president of the group during her last year as Long Beach's mayor — July 1, 2005, to June 30, 2006.

But before then, there was work to be done. Beverly had served as president of the California League of Cities as she ran for her third term, and one of her primary emphases was to stop the hemorrhaging of city tax revenues to state coffers. Another was the ongoing battle to get financial support for the cities' mandate to provide increased security in a post-9-11 world.

Beverly served on the national Homeland Security Task Force, raising at every opportunity how Long Beach (and Los Angeles) needed more help to protect its port — a likely target for terrorist acts. She also worked to tighten her already-close ties with California's senators, Diane Feinstein and Barbara Boxer. She first educated them about the great need, and then made sure Long Beach remained among their top priorities.

"We got great support from our senators," Beverly said. "It was our job to provide the support — the expertise and the facts — for them to use. We did that, and it worked."

Even though a Republican administration held the Washington purse strings now, Beverly and Port of Long Beach officials won several major grants to upgrade port security. Working with the city and the Port of Los Angeles, even more money was obtained for regional solutions such as a joint security command center.

Money woes at all levels — local, state and national — dominated the beginning of Beverly's third term.

In Long Beach, money proved to be the undoing of Henry Taboada as city manager. After he presented his proposed 2002-2003 budget in August, the City Council decided to ask him to leave. Beverly was unhappy, but tried to convince Taboada to resign. He declined, and the council ultimately ended his contract.

"She had a hard time understanding how they could treat a city manager that way," Jacobus said.

The one bright spot in the situation was that it put one of Beverly's first collaborators, Jerry Miller, into the seat as city manager. Beverly began working with Miller almost immediately to find a way out from under the $100 million+ deficit the city was facing.

The result was a three-year plan of structural changes in city government. While the plan itself was an accomplishment, the way it was formed provides another example of Beverly's quest for collaboration. For the first time, there was a citywide survey asking residents to help prioritize city services, and thereby pinpointing those places where cuts should come first. The survey was followed by public meetings before the budget was finalized to give yet another chance for the public to participate.

"Beverly drove the three-year plan," Miller said. "She wanted the community groups, the departments, etc., all involved in deciding priorities. She said 'do it this way.'

"We'd never done it this way before. But she was the one who said we had to do it in a completely open way."

It was Beverly's largest effort at collaboration — an entire city deciding how to cut its budget. Not everyone agreed with the final result, but no one could say they hadn't had a chance to participate. And the three-year plan received broad support.

"I honestly don't care who gets the credit in situations like this," Beverly says. "The important thing is to get it done, and get it done right."

Beverly's collaborative abilities were acknowledged again in 2003, when Republican Arnold Schwarzenegger named her to his transition team after his election as governor. That relationship would pay dividends quickly.

Schwarzenegger was elected as an alternative to Gray Davis, who was recalled in the same election. The movie star-turned-politician was elected as an economic reformer who pledged to balance the state budget without raising taxes.

But it appeared that the only way he could accomplish that was to raid local governments, either transferring tax revenues outright or requiring continuation of services while reducing or eliminating money for those services.

Eight of the 10 big city mayors came together to hammer out a proposal that would allow Schwarzenegger to balance that year's state budget while giving the cities relief from the never-ending state raids. The result was called Proposition 1A, which severely limited the state's ability to "borrow" revenue from local governments, and required repayment within a certain period of time.

"Proposition 1A was huge, historic," Miller said. "Essentially, we threw a Hail Mary pass. We were desperate. But Beverly got it done. She brought the mayors and the governor together and changed the state constitution with the proposition."

Beverly says the credit shouldn't go to her. All she did was bring the big city mayors together and worked with them.

Schwarzenegger not only agreed with the deal, he went out and campaigned for the proposition. At the same time, Beverly worked with Long Beach's state legislators to approve a side deal. Long Beach's portion of the state contribution would be paid through a 20-year, no-interest loan guaranteed by offshore Long Beach oil revenues.

"She won't admit it, but this was all Beverly's victory," Miller said. "She made it happen."

In the meantime, all those projects Beverly wanted to see through were becoming reality. The mixed-use CityPlace that re-placed the old Long Beach Plaza mall was completed in 2002. The next year, the Long Beach Unified School District won the Broad Prize as the best urban school district in the nation — a prize Beverly took great pleasure in talking about. The Pike at Rainbow Harbor complex, along with the first of the waterfront restaurants, opened in 2003. Equally important, the city opened its new, state-of-the-art 911 Emergency Command and Operations Center, as well as a new North Long Beach police substation.

CHAPTER **29**

The Nation's Mayor

Her tour as "the nation's mayor" actually began in mid-2005, but Beverly began preparing early. As the president-elect, she was very active with the U.S. Conference of Mayors. She had prepared an agenda that included an aggressive effort to bring the power of the nation's cities to bear on the complex and expensive problems being faced.

After effects of the 9-11 terrorists attacks still were being felt, both in the economic downturn and the need for increased security services. Then, on Aug. 28, 2005, Hurricane Katrina hit New Orleans and the Gulf Coast.

The coasts of two states were in disarray. New Orleans's mayor, Ray Nagin, was missing in action, and he and the city council were not communicating. Beverly knew it was her job to do something.

"Hurricane Katrina shaped Beverly's term as president of the U.S. Conference of Mayors," said Tom Cochran, executive director of the Conference of Mayors. "It was the most destructive national disaster this nation has ever seen. Shortly after it happened, we went to the Gulf Coast. She convened the first meeting of the mayors of Mississippi, and, with the assistance of Lt. Gov. Mitch Landrieu (who became mayor of New Orleans in 2010), brought about the first meeting of Mayor Ray Nagin and the New Orleans city council."

Proving once again that she is a leader focusing on what can be done, Beverly also came up with plans for concrete support. Through the Conference of Mayors, she instituted the adopt-a-city program where cities all across the country adopted cities and small towns devastated by the storm. Long Beach adopted Long Beach, Mississippi, and sent everything from money to books to restock the library to vehicles to replace some of those lost to Katrina.

The hurricane also gave Beverly another weapon in her arsenal for the fight to better equip cities as first responders to all forms of disaster. Using the tragedy in New Orleans as a primary example, she campaigned nationally for both monetary help and more user-friendly federal disaster regulations.

"We are facing the aftermath of a disaster the scope of which we simply weren't prepared for," she said in a speech after returning from her first post-hurricane trip. "And a lot of these things we need don't require money. They require the cutting of red tape."

Even with the huge distraction of Hurricane Katrina, Beverly held on to her overall national agenda. It is an approach she learned early on — from AA. You deal with the day's problems as they come, but you never stop working on the overall goal of staying sober.

Her program was called Cities for a Strong America. Noting that nearly half of the country's population lives in large metropolitan areas, she said that the mayors needed to both band together to make their issues known to the federal government and to take a more proactive approach to solving those problems.

The result was a series of four summits in a single year, spread throughout the country. An issue that is becoming increasingly urgent today, water supplies, was discussed in Albuquerque. A Denver summit addressed transportation issues, energy was discussed in Chicago and a summit in Los Angeles took on gangs.

At a speech to the National Press Club near the end of her

term as president of the conference, Beverly explained the emphasis this way.

"We have different problems, and we sometimes disagree, but in the end we mayors all face the same things, the same issues," she said. "At the end of the day, we all still have to take out the trash."

Beverly turned her attention outward, as well. She had emphasized Long Beach as the gateway to the Pacific Rim throughout her tenure as part of her promotion of trade, and she had already established some connections overseas. But as president of the conference, Beverly's reach became truly international.

As president of the conference, she led a delegation of mayors to China for the first-ever U.S.-China Mayors Summit. She went to Poland, where she quizzed mayors about how they had rebuilt their cities after the devastation of war — and used the insights to help the Gulf Coast cities. A trip to Ireland focused on education.

And she continued to break barriers. At an Asian Pacific Summit in Chouquing, China, she found herself the only woman on the podium. She also was the only woman from America at the 60th anniversary commemoration of the bombing of Hiroshima, placing a wreath on the monument honoring the dead. There are many benches in the park, but the one dedicated by the U.S. mayors delegation is the only one in English, and bears the names of Beverly O'Neill and Thomas Cochran.

"She's not just a national presence, she's an international presence," Charlotte, N.C., Mayor Patrick McCory said when Beverly completed her year as president. "You go to China and all they talk about is Beverly O'Neill. She's going to be a hard act to follow."

Cochran said Beverly had left something for the conference to build on — something she did everywhere she went.

"She not only made this organization stronger," Cochran said, "she set an agenda for making our cities stronger for generations to come."

It comes as no surprise that Beverly enjoyed making a difference for the country she loves. Wieder got to experience both the public triumphs and the private pleasure (and pain).

"Katrina shaped that year, but there were some incredible experiences with the Conference of Mayors," Wieder said. "She got to speak at the JFK Center (the John F. Kennedy School of Government at Harvard). She made a policy speech on urban renewal. Overall, she got to focus on what she did best. She was on the mountaintop until the day she left. There was no lame duck here."

Beverly's Legacy

Beverly O'Neill left the office of mayor of Long Beach on July 18, 2006. Some had asked her to run again, but she says she accomplished all she could. Others suggested her future was in an appointment in Washington, D.C., but she deflected those suggestions, saying she only wanted to live in Long Beach.

She remains active to this day, serving on a number of boards (a bank, a hospital, nonprofits) in the city as well as participation on national level commissions and committees. She and Bill enjoy a quiet life in their home on the beach, but Beverly still attends community functions and art performances frequently.

And that involvement truly is Beverly's legacy. She tells people that she loves Long Beach, that she wants to make it better, and then she goes out and does something about it. It just seems natural to follow her example.

Beverly was a trendsetter and a barrier breaker. But she did it with style and grace.

"She remained a lady no matter what situation she was in," Bill Barnes said. "She was not a woman trying to be a man. And for her, the stakes were never so high to cause her to compromise her basic beliefs.

"She's wise in the best sense of the word. If I were going to do something challenging, I would consult with her. Whether she agreed with me or not, I would be benefited by her advice. She is something special."

Her beliefs came from a childhood that forced Beverly to rely on God and her mother. Her mother and AA added both the compassion and the strength to deal with difficult situations humanely. Moreover, the AA philosophy of supporting and accepting support point directly to Beverly's emphasis on collaboration and focus on facilitating instead of commanding.

"When I started, I was worried that the city needed a table-pounder, and that's not me," Beverly said. "I was a facilitative leader. It takes a lot longer, but in the end there is a better understanding of why you made the decision. I wanted to be a visible mayor, a mayor who let people know what they were doing was appreciated."

Years after her tenure as mayor, Beverly continues to inspire standing ovations at events. She continues to inspire loyalty — by earning it.

Chris Garner, the well-spoken director of the Gas and Oil Department for the city, tried to explain her impact at her retirement party.

"You have impacted so many of our lives in a manner far beyond that associated with simply being mayor," he said. "We loved your continually upbeat personality, your words of encouragement and support, your relentless energy, your ever-present smile, your kindness, your enthusiasm, your patience and your always evident love for Long Beach. All of these qualities were contagious and raised the awareness of residents, employees and visitors as to what a special place Long Beach is to live, work and play."

U,S. Sen. Diane Feinstein credits Beverly with making a huge difference in Long Beach's direction.

"I have known Beverly for more than two decades and without a doubt, Long Beach's success is a testament to her tremendous

CHAPTER 30 — BEVERLY'S LEGACY ⮞

work and leadership," she said. "From her noteworthy election as a write-in candidate to her 12 years as mayor, Beverly has established herself as an institution in her own right."

Beverly acknowledges that her 12 years as mayor were momentous ones. As you would expect, she credits those around her instead of her leadership.

"We totally remade our city because we had to," she said. "There was no choice."

Some go so far as to say that there really was no choice when it came to Beverly being mayor.

"She was a gift to Long Beach," Jerry Miller said. "I don't usually think much of things like destiny, but if anyone was destined to be mayor at a certain time, it was her. She was destined to lead this city out of chaos."

Looking in from the outside, Mike Murray offered the mayor the highest compliment, saying she wasn't like other politicians. He ended that retirement party with a simple statement.

"Thank you, Mayor O'Neill, for giving all of us a sense of worth," he said.

Giving people a sense of worth — a noble goal, and a goal Beverly lived, start to finish. She began as a child, helping a beleaguered mother. She learned from that same mother, and AA, how to value an individual even while you help them — often helping simply by valuing.

She provided generations of women and students with a sense of worth through her work at Long Beach City College. She gave Long Beach hope in the darkest of times, convincing the city that it was worth doing the work it would take to come out the other side. Then she facilitated that change.

She always had a smile and a kind word. She succeeded as a leader in Long Beach because no one could doubt that her only motivation was her love and caring for the city and its people.

She was, from start to finish, passionately positive.

Acknowledgements

Thank you first and foremost to Beverly O'Neill, who gave generously of her time and insight. Her true humility sometimes made it difficult to convince her to give proper perspective to the role she played, but her gentleness and humor made the process ever enjoyable.

A number of people offered information, recollection and different points of view. Key among them were Jerry Miller, Diane Jacobus, Cathy Wieder and Jim Hankla. All were instrumental parts of Beverly's years as mayor, and were generous in their time and recollections. Thanks also to Wells Sloniger, who shed light on Beverly's maturation at Long Beach City College.

A special thanks to Judy Seal, who not only offered her own unique experiences with Beverly, but also acted as editor, sounding board and advisor. Her encouragement, along with Mike Murray's, kept the book alive when it could have easily died.

I would be remiss if I didn't thank my wife, Maria, for putting up with many nights of a husband sequestered in another room, or preoccupied with what had to seem at times nothing but a dream.

Finally, thank you, dear reader, for taking the time to peruse this effort. It is my prayer that you have found it a positive experience — maybe even passionately positive.

Breinigsville, PA USA
01 October 2010
246545BV00001B/3/P